Find the Job You've Always Wanted *in Half the Time with Half the Effort*

Find the Job You've Always Wanted *in Half the Time with Half the Effort*

Jeffrey J. Mayer

CB

CONTEMPORARY
BOOKS

Library of Congress Cataloging-in-Publication Data

Mayer, Jeffrey J.
   Find the job you've always wanted in half the time with
half the effort / Jeffrey J. Mayer.
      p.   cm.
   ISBN 0-8092-3917-5 (cloth)
       0-8092-3816-0 (paper)
    1. Job hunting.   2. Job hunting—United
States.   I. Title.
HF5382.7.M39   1992
650.14—dc20   91-48177
                                        CIP

Published by Contemporary Books, Inc.
180 North Michigan Avenue, Chicago, Illinois 60601
Manufactured in the United States of America
International Standard Book Number: 0-8092-3917-5 (cloth)
                                          0-8092-3816-0 (paper)

To my wife, Mitzi, and my daughter, DeLaine,
both of whom I love very much

Contents

Acknowledgments

This book would never have been written were it not for the encouragement and guidance of my literary agent, Lois de la Haba. Lois, thank you for all your contributions to my literary career.

Harvey Plotnick, my publisher and editor, and Julie Walski, his senior vice president and associate publisher, have helped shape my ideas for this book into a polished manuscript. Harvey and Julie, I couldn't have done this without your help and assistance, for which I am very grateful.

And finally, I would like to thank the following people, who graciously agreed to speak with me about my book: Charles Cone, Jr., Mihaly Csikszentmihalyi, Robert M. Goss, Theodore L. Gross, Joel Hochberg, Robert J. Kelly, Judith L. Lansky, Camille Lavington, Dr. Tim Mescon, Ben T. Nelson, Arthur S. Nicholas, Daniel O'Connell, James A. Paglia, Cynthia Rapponotti, Katherine Louise Ross, Brad Saul, Frederick I. Schick, Joyce L. Watts, Barry Wolf, and Gary M. Wolfson.

Find the Job You've Always Wanted *in Half the Time with Half the Effort*

An Overview

Finding the job that's right for you is a step-by-step process. With my Career Discovery System, you'll start by setting aside some quiet time and answering some important questions about yourself and your work. The answers to these questions will help you quickly pinpoint what you like, what's important to you, and what you do well. You will use this information when you write your resume and will refer to it again during your preparation for your job interviews. Next this book will show you how to identify, contact, and schedule appointments with potential employers. And, finally, we will discuss how to negotiate a job offer and offer suggestions on how you can make your new career more enjoyable and rewarding.

You'll get the most benefit from the book by first reading it from beginning to end without stopping. This will provide you with an overview of my Career Discovery System and the opportunity to see how it works. Don't be afraid to write in this book—it's yours. Read with a pen, pencil, or highlighter in your hand. If an idea occurs to you, write it in the margin or on a separate piece of paper. Highlight or underline words or paragraphs that you think will be helpful when you go back and do the work step-by-step. Then it will be easy for you to quickly locate the specific pages that you feel are important to review.

1
Preparing to Find Your New Job

The time has come to look for a new job. The problem is *we don't know how*!

We've all invested years of our lives learning our business or profession, but we've spent very little time learning how to find a new job, especially one that is emotionally and professionally fulfilling as well as financially rewarding. We don't know how to organize our thoughts, we don't know how to write a resume that will get us interviews, and we don't know how to sell ourselves to a potential employer.

There are countless individual reasons why people look for better jobs, but the one thing we all have working against us is *time*. The longer we search, the more taxing it is on our emotions and our finances. We need to discover a better method of determining what we really *want* in a career. We should be looking for positions that will utilize our skills, talents, creativity, and ingenuity. Life doesn't begin at 5:00 P.M. on Friday and end at 9:00 A.M. Monday.

It takes skill, practice, and patience to go out and find a new job. For most of us, this is a chore we don't look forward to. We're out of practice, feel insecure, and are faced with the challenge of doing something we never did very well.

Don't Believe Everything You Read

Newspapers and magazines tend to publish two types of feature stories about people who are looking for jobs. The first is the "I Am the Victim" article, which describes how difficult it is to find a job. These are stories about people who are unemployed and unable to find work or people who feel trapped in their jobs and don't know how to escape. The articles frequently quote career consultants who describe the tight job market and advise, "For each $10,000 of annual salary an applicant will typically spend a month searching for a new position." That means the search will take six months for a $60,000 salary and fifteen months for a salary of $150,000. This is crazy!

The other type of article tells us that by taking additional courses or earning another advanced degree we'll become much more qualified for a better position. These discussions offer only external judgments about how to succeed. They put a lot of pressure on us to engage in expensive activities that have nothing to do with who we are as individuals, what we value, what we're committed to accomplishing in our careers, or even our basic interests. Just because everybody else has an MBA does not mean you should go out and get one. Just because a major business magazine, newspaper, or politician declares that _____ is the next "hot" career, it doesn't mean you should drop everything you've been doing to run after it. A career field that people view as a sure thing because an industry is booming at a given time may a few short years later turn out to be nothing more than a fad. In the early 1980s, for instance, when oil prices were sky-high and the industry was flourishing, everyone with the remotest mechanical bent dashed off to places like Carnegie-Mellon University for the credentials they thought they'd need to cash in on the trend. By the time they'd earned their degrees in petroleum engineering, though, the oil boom was over and the majority of the nation's petroleum engineers were unemployed. By the mid-1980s investment banking had become the hot career. However, the people who flocked to business schools as a result of *that* fad graduated at the beginning of the 1990s just as Wall Street was initiating massive layoffs.

The point is things change, often very quickly. A fad by definition is short-lived. Once you hear about it, it's usually peaked and may already be over. If you try to chart your career by chasing bandwagons, you'll almost certainly be disappointed.

If additional classes will truly help your career, do consider taking them. But don't enroll until you're certain that the commitment of time and expense will repay you with the expected rewards.

A Typical Job Search

You're reading this book because you've decided it's time to look for a new job. Something has happened to make you decide to leave your present employer, or you're out of work and need to find a job in a hurry. How do you go about searching for this new position? What should you do first? How can you reduce the time and effort most people say it takes to find a job?

If you're like most people, you'll pull out your old resume, the one you most recently updated several years ago, and add a few new bits of employment information. You'll contact some friends and business associates, answer newspaper advertisements, and send the same resume and cover letter to hundreds of different people.

As the days and weeks go by, you'll sit next to the phone, waiting for someone to call and invite you in for an interview. You'll receive preprinted rejection letters instead. They will all read the same: "Thank you for your interest in our company. Unfortunately, we have no positions available at this time. We will, however, keep your resume on file should an opening occur." That is, if you receive a response at all.

Needless to say, after mailing dozens or even hundreds of these letters without receiving even a single invitation for an interview, you'll become depressed and despondent. You will run out of leads. You'll become resigned to the belief that there aren't any jobs out there. You will have squandered your most precious assets—a lot of your time, a great deal of energy, and possibly part of your savings.

This is how we've been taught to look for a job. Everybody uses the same approach, from corporate managers to college graduates. Our cover letters are frequently addressed simply to a position or title, "President," or "Vice President of Human Resources." Too often we don't take the time to learn what these companies do, who these people are, or even the correct spelling of their names. Lots of hard work and energy are wasted without getting any results. We're doing it the wrong way.

My Career Discovery System will help you combine the values that are important to you with the type of work you do best and the activities you enjoy most. It will help get you organized, show you how to discover what you like, and help you identify your most marketable skills and talents. I'll share with you my proven techniques for finding potential employers, and I will show you how to contact them and schedule appointments so that you'll be meeting with people who are interested in hiring you instead of sitting by the telephone waiting for someone to respond to a recently mailed resume. You'll develop the tools you need to go out, sell yourself, and find the job you've always wanted.

Look at the Odds

Try to imagine the office of a person to whom you're mailing your resume. Put yourself in that position for a few minutes. The desk is covered with piles of letters, memos, and reports. In one corner is an in basket holding a huge stack of resumes. (Many corporate executives receive more than a hundred *unsolicited* resumes each month.) Do you have any idea how many people saw that advertisement in the local paper, the *Wall Street Journal*, or the Sunday *New York Times* and decided to send in a resume? There could be hundreds or even a thousand responses!

Some of these people, yourself included, may indeed be qualified for the job; but how much time do you think this overworked corporate vice president is

able to spend on each letter or resume that arrives
when there isn't enough time to complete the regular
day's work?

There are so many resumes to review that it's
very difficult to separate the wheat from the chaff,
especially during regular business hours. So the executive stuffs this huge pile of papers in a briefcase and
takes it home. After dinner, while sitting in a comfortable chair in front of the television, the executive
begins to sift and sort. Each letter is scanned for
perhaps five to ten seconds and searched for something attention-getting. If that something appears, the
letter is placed in a keeper pile for further consideration. The rest get reject letters.

The odds obviously aren't in your favor. When
there are so many applicants, it's difficult to make
yourself stand out in the crowd. To make matters
worse, the person making the hiring decision is most
likely tired and worn out. This is not an enjoyable
job. Looking through piles of resumes, meeting with
applicants, and finally negotiating the terms of employment is an exhausting and time-consuming process.

With the enormous competition for jobs in today's business environment, you're not being realistic
or honest with yourself if you think you'll be successful in your job search simply by mailing out resumes.
Quite often the position being advertised isn't even
truly available. It's already been filled, the company
only going through the motions of advertising to
comply with corporate policy, state laws, or other
regulations that require it to make job openings
known to the general public.

My Career Discovery System will show you how

to become more creative and resourceful in locating available jobs. You'll learn how to improve your odds of getting the job you *really want*. There are better and more effective ways to market and sell yourself to potential employers than by answering blind newspaper advertisements and mailing letters cold.

Why I Wrote This Book

Many of the ideas, techniques, and strategies in this book come from my own career experiences as well as the experiences and observations of the corporate executives and businesspeople I've worked with during the past twenty years. I've learned there's always a world of new career opportunities out there, calling for a wide variety of skills and talents. But you must go out and look for them.

My own business career started in 1972 when I went to work in my father's property and casualty insurance agency after college. In 1973 he passed away and I inherited the business. However, I soon realized I didn't like running the agency, and I negotiated its sale in 1976.

I then became a special agent with Northwestern Mutual Life. I thought I would enjoy a career helping people find solutions to their business, financial, and estate-planning problems, and I did it for eight years. During those years I learned and developed new skills and improved the talents I was blessed with. I learned how to meet people and how to use the telephone to schedule appointments with them, and I improved my organizational skills.

By 1984 I realized my calling in life wasn't in financial planning. I was struggling to find an answer

to the question, "What am I going to do with the rest
of my life?" I was thirty-four years old, divorced, and
looking for a change. I began to ask myself questions.
What was I good at? What did I enjoy doing? What
were my skills and talents? I realized that one
strength stood out above the others: I was organized.
I had learned how to use my time effectively and, as
a result, I did my work well and got it done on time
with a minimum of effort. Over the years I had developed a fabulous system for handling paperwork. My
clean-desk approach saved me time and improved my
productivity immensely.

I decided to start a consulting firm to teach busy
people how to get organized, save time, and make
more money by working more productively. My spe-
cialty became cleaning up the office. I would take a
desk that looked as if it had gone through the spin
cycle of a washing machine, with piles of paper ev-
erywhere, and in two hours transform that desktop
into one that looked like the flight deck of an aircraft
carrier. I quickly became the highest-paid executive
efficiency expert in the country, earning up to $300 an
hour.

USA Today dubbed me "Mr. Neat, the Clutter-
buster," *People* magazine called me "the Power Desk
Cleaner to Corporate America," and the *Chicago Sun-
Times* referred to me as "the World's Most Expensive
Maid."

My business was successful because I utilized
the skills I had learned earlier in my career: how to
search for people I thought would have an interest in
my services and how to effectively work the telephone to land appointments with them. I realized that
everything we learn is portable—we take it with us

wherever we go. The things we learned yesterday make us much more valuable tomorrow.

You Call the Shots

Employment is no longer a cradle-to-grave experience. The days of working at the same company for twenty-five or thirty years are long gone.

In today's economic climate, we can't leave our careers to chance. The quality of our lives and our family's financial and emotional well-being are too important. Just as we purchase insurance to protect us in the event of an economic loss or disaster, we should also take the time to prepare for the possibility of being out of work.

There's no way of knowing what may happen in the future. You could pick up the morning newspaper and learn that your company has been acquired over the weekend. Your situation has changed dramatically as a result. You may still have a job, but because of the administrative or personnel changes you no longer enjoy working there. You're squeezed between a rock and a hard place. The thought of leaving makes you extremely uncomfortable, but staying is no longer a pleasant experience. You feel trapped.

Life is too short to spend eight, ten, or twelve hours a day doing something you don't enjoy or working in an office environment where you aren't comfortable or sufficiently challenged. If you're counting the days until the next holiday, it's time to start looking for a new job. It isn't a catastrophe to discover you don't like your job. It's only a tragedy when you stay there. You don't necessarily have to do the same kind of work in the future that you've done in the past. Don't be afraid to do something new for yourself. This could be your opportunity to find a new, more enjoyable, line of work. The majority of us spend years searching for our niche. Keep looking until you find yours. Be flexible in your career thinking and planning. Prepare for the unexpected.

Start by changing the way you view yourself and your career. It's up to you to take care of yourself. No corporation will look after you.

Look at your career in three- to five-year periods. Most people need to make some kind of job change at these intervals because they've mastered their responsibilities and need new challenges. Start by showing your employer that your presence is making a difference. Demonstrate how valuable you are and that you're making big contributions to the organization. If your employer doesn't recognize or appreciate all you have to offer, you have the knowledge and confidence that you can go out and find another position in weeks instead of months.

Wherever you go, whatever you do, the skills and talents you've developed come along with you. The knowledge, training, and experience you've received will make you even more valuable to a new employer at a new company.

2
Take Control
of Your Career

If You Lose Your Job, Don't Panic

Losing a job can be a devastating experience, especially if you weren't prepared for it. Expect to go through a period of mourning or grieving. For some people the loss of a job can feel nearly as devastating as the loss of a loved one. Surround yourself with people who will encourage you. The support of your family and friends will help you get through this difficult period. Participate in activities that lift your spirits. Create a support system of friends who will tell you how good you are, help you see that there are opportunities and options available, and remind you that there is hope for the future.

Don't spend your time with people who complain about how terrible things are. Don't sit around feeling sorry for yourself, but do give yourself time to work through these emotions. Take as much time as you need to get your confidence back. Develop an attitude that you're worthy and valuable. Create a positive atmosphere and environment for yourself. You must believe there is light at the end of the tunnel.

Benefits You're Entitled To

If you've just been terminated, sit down with your employer and see what kind of severance benefits you're entitled to or can negotiate. You may receive some extra benefits simply because you took the time to ask.

Will the firm continue paying your salary, or a portion of it, for a specific period of time? Try to get them to pay your medical and life insurance premiums, or a portion of them, for at least six months. This could save you hundreds of dollars a month. Federal law, through COBRA (the Consolidated Omnibus Budget Reconciliation Act), guarantees that companies with twenty or more employees allow you to continue your present medical insurance benefits; however, you will be responsible for paying the entire premium plus a small charge for administrative costs. You will have to decide if the continuation of this coverage is less expensive than purchasing your own individual policy.

Would the company provide you with outplacement counseling? Could you continue to use an office, a telephone, and secretarial assistance? Could you get a contract to do some consulting work for the firm?

Depending on your specific circumstances, you may wish to contact a lawyer, an accountant, or an employee benefits consultant. Don't rely entirely upon the personnel department at your former company for advice. They may not be able to give you the best advice. They are trained to answer questions specific to the company only, and they work for the company, not for you.

Income Continuation

You'll most likely continue to receive some income for a brief period of time, either from a salary continuation plan or from unemployment compensation benefits, so make the most of the extra breathing room. Cut your costs and living expenses to the bare minimum. Create a leaner monthly budget. (Creating a budget is discussed in Chapter 4.) Put your credit cards away or cut them up, and don't make any unnecessary purchases.

If your financial situation is not as healthy as you'd like or if your peace of mind would benefit from knowing you have a little more breathing room, don't be afraid to work with your creditors. Contact the people to whom you owe money and try to work out easier payment terms. You can probably arrange new terms on your mortgage, loan payments, and the outstanding balances on your credit cards.

Don't allow your salary continuation program or unemployment compensation to create a sense of security. It will be false security. Don't spend your severance pay on a vacation! If you do, you'll wind up with no source of income before you've even begun your job search. Then you'll have to deplete your savings or investments to cover your living expenses. You've worked too hard to accumulate that money. It wasn't put away with the idea that it would be spent on the mortgage and food. You put it away for that trip you've always dreamed of taking, your children's education, or a nest egg for your retirement. Pretend this money doesn't exist. This will force you to look for a new job before touching your savings.

Losing your job could even turn out to be a blessing in disguise. If you weren't fully satisfied with your old job, this will compel you to go out and find something that will be more rewarding and fulfilling. My Career Discovery System will make the process of finding a new position easier and faster because it offers a logical and systematic approach. Once you start following it, you'll discover that there are many opportunities available. You may awaken your entrepreneurial spirit and decide that this is the time to start your own business, or to market the skills you've developed to other companies as a business consultant. Everybody can find a new job. It may not necessarily be the same type of work you did in the past, but frequently you'll wind up earning even more than you did before.

Prepare Your Plan of Action

Most people approach the search for a job backward. They spend their time, effort, and a great deal of money searching for a job, but they don't invest more than a few minutes thinking about it and preparing their plan of action. As a consequence, they have poor results. Weeks and months pass, while they're still seeking that elusive job because they didn't know precisely what they were searching for in the first place.

Before you start making telephone calls or mailing out resumes, set aside some private time and give yourself the opportunity to think about your goals, dreams, and desires. Spend time searching for answers to these questions: Who am I? What do I want? And why do I want it?

The time you spend thinking, planning, and identifying what's important to you will save you time in the long run by making it much easier to find the job *you* want.

With today's ever-increasing work loads, we tend to spend the majority of our waking hours *doing* our work rather than studying how to function more successfully within our jobs or how to find better ones. By taking the time to explore what you want and need, your chances of making a better career decision will be greatly improved.

The first step in the Career Discovery System is to pinpoint what you really want, the kind of position you would find fulfilling, and the type of business organization you'll be comfortable working in. You will create your own plan of action.

Depending on your situation, your job search falls into one of two categories:

- You have a job but are looking for something different.
- You're out of work and need to find something immediately.

If you're currently working, you must set aside a portion of your personal time to design a plan of action for your next career move.

If you're out of work, you will feel a sense of urgency about your job search. For you this project will become your full-time job—not just for two or three days a week or three or four hours a day, but five days a week, eight or more hours a day.

Steps to Take if You're About to Lose Your Job

Most people go into shock when they learn they've lost their job, even when they didn't like it. If you suspect your employment situation might change suddenly, prepare a contingency plan.

If you think that your position may be in jeopardy, make copies of the papers, names, or telephone numbers you'll need should you be forced to start a new job search. If you've been keeping personal papers or other information at the office, transfer that information to your home also. Some employers take the position that everything in your office is company property, even your Rolodex, and you may find that you no longer have access to any of it when they let you go.

Create a list of all the contacts you've made over the years. Throughout your career you've come in contact with hundreds of people. Some of them could become future job resources, sources for leads, or contacts for interviews.

3
Reduce the Time and Effort of Your Job Search

Maximize Your Time

When you wake up each morning, ask yourself, "What will I do today to help further my goal of getting a job?" Time is the most valuable asset you have. It can't be replaced. You'll need time to yourself, and a schedule and a routine to follow every day, just as if you were going to the office. Continue to remind yourself that you have only one goal and objective: *to get the job you want.*

Overcome Inertia

The hardest thing for any of us to do is get started. It's far too easy to sit down and think about all the things we should be doing without ever doing any of them. Once you get started on your job search you'll begin to develop momentum, which will keep you energized and excited. A big project is nothing more than the completion of many smaller projects. It's like eating an apple. You can't eat the whole thing in one bite, but if you take one small bite, and then another and another, before you know it, the apple's gone.

Stay Focused

To remain focused on your job search, you need to be disciplined. When you know what you want to accomplish, you won't allow yourself to be distracted. Break your longer-term goals into daily objectives. Ask yourself, "What do I have to do today to achieve my goal?" Break it down even further. "What should I be doing this morning? This afternoon?"

Put your plan in writing. Make an outline for yourself, and always give yourself a deadline. Try to stay ahead of schedule so that you can not only reach your goal but beat it. Review your progress on a daily basis and, to keep everything in perspective, look at your plan before you go to bed at night and again when you get up in the morning.

Once a week take some time to think about your original goals and objectives, and list all the things you've accomplished this past week. Be proud of how much you've achieved in such a short period of time. It won't be a catastrophe if you haven't achieved all of the things you set out to do, but give yourself credit for the things you did complete. Your objective is to move forward. Is your glass half-empty or half-full?

Take pride in your successes. Give yourself a big pat on the back for a job well done. Maybe you've even earned the reward of a dinner out.

During your job search other things will continue

to come into the picture, and naturally demand some of your time and attention. You can't allow yourself to stray too far off track, however, or alter your activities so much that you're going in the wrong direction. You must always keep that big picture in mind.

Start Your Day with a Bang

We all have a time of day when we do our best work. For most of us that occurs during the morning hours. We're fresh, alert, and energetic, and our ability to concentrate is excellent. During your job search start each day with a bang. Use the morning hours to tackle your most difficult projects. You'll find you become twice as productive with half the effort. Create a schedule that allows for a productive morning *every* morning. The energy and enthusiasm you develop will carry you through the afternoon. In the same way, when you have a productive Monday, you'll find the entire week is rewarding and fulfilling.

To guarantee that you use your time most effectively, plan your schedule for tomorrow before you finish working tonight. When you start work in the morning, you'll be mentally prepared for the projects you plan to tackle.

Some people are in the habit of starting their day by doing the easy tasks first. They think this will somehow get them in the right mood for doing the important, difficult, time-consuming ones. Unfortunately, it doesn't work that way. They waste their time and energy on insignificant, trivial tasks, and by the time they finally start on something important and meaningful, they're exhausted.

Schedule an Appointment with Yourself

One sure way to guarantee you'll get to your important work is to schedule an appointment with yourself. You've scheduled meetings with other people day in and day out throughout your career. Now block out some time for you, and you'll get your work done on time.

Write these appointments in your calendar, and keep them. Close the door, turn off the telephone so you won't be interrupted, and go to work. Be specific about what you're planning to do: write letters, make telephone calls, work on your resume. When you've completed one project, go on to the next step in your action plan for getting a new job.

Many times we underestimate the amount of time needed to complete a project, so always allow yourself some extra time. As a general rule, increase the amount of time you think you'll need by 50 percent. If you think you'll need an hour, block out an hour and a half instead.

At the end of the day, try to do at least one more thing before calling it quits. Make one more telephone call, or write one more sentence or paragraph of a letter. Get into the habit of cleaning up and organizing your office or work space before you stop in the evening so you'll be ready to jump right in when you begin again in the morning. Think of that old proverb—don't put off until tomorrow that which you can do now.

You'll need privacy in order to think and concentrate with a minimal number of interruptions. If you're at home, that means closing the door and asking family members to leave you alone for at least a few hours at a time.

If you can't work at home, find somewhere else to go. Perhaps you can use an empty desk at your previous place of work, or maybe you know somebody who would let you use an office and a phone on a temporary basis. If you're unable to find a quiet place to work, go to the public library. Your objective is to establish a routine, just as if you were going to the office. Whether you're working at home or out of the house, you need to be at your desk doing something constructive by 9:00 A.M. every morning.

These productivity-improving techniques will help keep you on track and on target as you work through the Career Discovery System.

Write Everything Down

Don't keep all your thoughts in your head. Use a pencil and paper instead. Create a Master List to keep track of all the things you must do or follow up on every day. You'll find that by keeping a written inventory of all your unfinished work, you won't need to remember quite as much.

Use a big piece of paper or a tablet for your Master List, not the back of an envelope or a Post-it note. Write on every line, don't worry about priorities, and don't number the items. After you've filled up the first page, start a second one. When you've completed about 50 percent of the work on page one, transfer and consolidate the remaining work onto the newest page and throw the old page away. Review your Master List throughout the day, and ask yourself, "What's the most important project I must work on now?" Then set aside some time and do it.

With the creation of your Master List you'll be able to file or toss most of the papers and files that have been piled on your desk, because they were left there simply to remind you to write a letter, make a telephone call, or do something else. For a more detailed and thorough description of how to get organized and improve your productivity, pick up a copy of my book *If You Haven't Got the Time to Do It Right, When Will You Find the Time to Do It Over?* (Simon and Schuster).

4
The Career Discovery System

Decide What It Is *You* Want

Before you even begin to think about writing your resume or making telephone calls to friends or associates, you've got to spend some time thinking about yourself. Sometimes we've run so hard to keep up with the competition that we don't know who we are anymore. The purpose of this self-evaluation is to help you get to know yourself better. Let's take a few minutes to ask ourselves some probing questions and use the opportunity to rediscover what's important to us and what we want to do with our lives. As you spend the following days searching and exploring, you'll be trying to put many things into their proper perspective. What do you like? What do you value? What's important to you? What do the members of your family value, and how does that relate to you? How do you communicate with people? How do you express yourself? How do you make decisions? Your answers will give you the ability to focus on the things that are most important and provide you with some parameters. With this information it becomes easier to make decisions about your job search.

Don't be surprised if this is difficult at first. Stick with it. A good way to start is by writing whatever thoughts cross your mind—free-form thinking. Don't worry about what you're writing. There are no right or wrong answers. Just be honest with yourself. You'll have the opportunity to refine your thoughts as you go along. The information you'll be accumulating will help you identify the skills, talents, and accomplishments you can offer a new employer. Your research will also serve as a basis from which to write your resume.

During your self-evaluation, try to imagine what new types of jobs or lines of work you would enjoy. What kinds of businesses or industries do you find fascinating? What size organization do you think you would be most comfortable in? What type of corporate structure feels right to you—a large structured corporation or a small entrepreneurial one?

Ask yourself a lot of questions. Really probe and challenge yourself. Write all your thoughts and ideas down and date every page, so you can look back and see where your thoughts fell chronologically.

Organize your notes inside properly labeled file folders, so you'll be able to find them later. Use new manila file folders, and make a separate folder for every topic or category that comes to mind: types of jobs; types of companies, businesses, or organizations; preferred locations; and anything else you think of. Write the name of the file on the tab and use a fine-tipped pen (pencils smudge and become illegible).

Don't write about more than one subject, idea, or

thought on the same piece of paper. If you do, you may find that you can't decide where the sheet belongs. It will end up in one of the piles on your desk and will be ultimately lost and forgotten. Continue to refresh your memory by reviewing your notes frequently. As new thoughts occur, write them down and file them in the appropriate file.

On the following pages, you'll be asked to make lists on a number of different topics. Each list stands alone, although you'll quickly discover that some of the same points will appear on more than one list. The overlapping items will help you to identify specific skills, talents, or interests on which you should begin to focus. You'll quickly notice you're crystallizing your thinking.

Start with Work You Enjoy

Make a list of all the aspects of your latest job that you enjoyed. What did you like? Think about all the tasks, responsibilities, and projects you worked on during the past months or years that were satisfying and fulfilling.

Don't stop with a list of five or ten items. Write down *everything*. Work on this list during several sessions over the course of a few days. Don't be in a hurry. Make this a fun project by turning it into something you enjoy. By the time you've finished, you could easily have a list of thirty, fifty, even a hundred items. You had your job for XX years, and worked within the industry for YY years—there should be some pretty powerful reasons why you stayed there. What were they?

Now, think about your prior jobs and ask yourself the same questions. This will give you an overview of everything you've enjoyed in your entire career. When you're doing something you like, you're probably also good at it. Make a folder labeled *Work I Enjoy*.

Change What Doesn't Suit You

In every job there are things that you love and enjoy, and there are other aspects you dislike or absolutely hate. So make another list of everything you didn't like about your job, your company, and your industry. There's a pretty good chance you can come up with a very long list. Write everything down and put it aside for a day.

Now rewrite your list, rephrasing each negative item into a positive statement. For example: "I spent too much time out of town and away from home" would become "I want a job where I don't travel so much."

This will give you additional useful information about yourself, helping you pinpoint what you really enjoy doing and what type of organization you want to become a part of. Put your list in a file labeled *Things to Change*.

Refine Your *Work I Enjoy* List
Go through your *Work I Enjoy* list and narrow it down to about twenty items, keeping the activities that you liked the most.

Identify Your *Skills and Talents*

What do you like to do? What are you good at doing? What kinds of things are you able to do easily and effortlessly? What do you really enjoy? What gives you pleasure? If you had more time, what would you do with it? If you didn't have to work, how would you spend your time?

Pull out your yellow pad and start writing. Write down everything that comes to mind, including your hobbies and outside interests. Many people have been able to turn hobbies or outside interests into very successful businesses. Put your list in a file labeled *Skills and Talents*.

Refine Your *Things to Change* List

Go through your *Things to Change* list and shorten it to about twenty items, keeping the items you feel are most important.

Add Up Your *Accomplishments*

What have been your major accomplishments during your career? What were you commended for during your performance appraisals? What projects can you look back on and say, "I did a good job!" What are you most proud of? Think in terms of specific accomplishments, not the job titles you've held. If your job was as a financial analyst, and you write down "I was successful at analyzing financial statements," that doesn't say enough. Dig deeper. What did the analysis deal with? Be specific.

Maybe you analyzed potential corporate acquisitions, searching through balance sheets and financial reports for undiscovered "gems." That indicates that you like to dig into new things, things you knew nothing about before you got started. Remember the time you were a corporate hero because you found some hidden information that revealed that the company you were studying was underpriced and therefore a good acquisition candidate? Or when you were commended for discovering some skeletons in a company's closet and the board of directors decided to follow your recommendation to take a pass on the acquisition, saving a lot of money as a result? If one of your accomplishments was interviewing people, that makes you an investigator, a compiler of information. Making recommendations makes you a strategist, a decision maker, a big-picture thinker.

Describe what you've done in the past and what you're capable of doing in the future. Give yourself credit for your accomplishments in an open and honest manner. Put your list in a file labeled *Accomplishments*.

Refine Your *Skills and Talents* List

Go through your *Skills and Talents* list and shorten it to about twenty items. Then put your lists aside for a few days to give yourself a chance to think about them.

Analyze How You Landed Your Previous Jobs

Think back to the circumstances that led you to take your most recent job. How were you introduced to the firm? What were the specific reasons why you took this position? What, or who, made the biggest impression on you? How has the company changed since you began working there? If you're still there, why do you want to leave? What were the reasons why you took your other previous jobs?

How have your personal circumstances changed since you started working? What's changed about your life? Family responsibilities? Financial needs? Your goals and dreams? Are the things that were important to you in the past still as important to you now? Are there events that have changed the course of your career? Make a file labeled *How I Got My Previous Jobs*.

Refine Your Lists

Now return to your *Work I Enjoy* and *Things to Change* lists and shorten each to about twelve items.

Now go through the *Skills and Talents* and *Accomplishments* lists and narrow each list down to about twelve items.

Rank Your Priorities

If you have difficulty deciding which of the items should be included in your shortened lists, give yourself more time to think about them. You may find this priority comparison method helpful.

Write your undecided items in any order on a numbered list:

1. _____   3. _____

2. _____   4. _____

Now choose the most important item by deciding between the items in pairs, as follows, and on your list put a check mark beside your choice:

1 or 2, 1 or 3, 1 or 4

2 or 3, 2 or 4

3 or 4

The item that has the most check marks is the most important to you.

Identify the People You Admire Most

Who are two or three of the most remarkable people you've ever met or read about? Why? What qualities and characteristics do you admire most? What contributions have these people made? How could you emulate them or follow their paths? Which of their qualities do you see in yourself? Write all this down. Put it in a file labeled *People I Admire*.

Pinpoint What You're Working Toward

When your career is over, what would you like to see when you look back? Do you want to leave behind some accomplishments that would be remembered by others? Do you want to move up to a position where you have influence and power over the future of an organization? Do you want to influence people's careers and lives, making your contribution by helping them grow and develop? What are you looking for beyond financial security and stability? What will keep you interested and stimulated? What will generate excitement and enthusiasm for you?

Determine the Meaning of Money

Is money a yardstick by which you measure your success? Do you use it to compare yourself with others? Do you think of it as a tool that buys time and a higher standard of living? Are you motivated by the accumulation of wealth, power, or fame? Will more money make you more comfortable, happier, or feel better about yourself? What does money mean to you?

How much money do you *really* need to support your lifestyle? When was the last time you sat down and worked out a monthly budget? You may find it helpful to calculate the base salary figure you actually need, and then a wish-list figure, which would cover things you haven't been able to afford.

Monthly Expenses

Auto Expenses _____

Auto Loan _____

Bank Charges _____

Charitable Donations _____

Child Care Expenses _____

Clothing _____

Credit Card Payments _____

Dining Out _____

Education _____

    Self _____

    Children _____

Groceries _____

Home Repair and Maintenance _____

Insurance   _____

Interest Expense   _____

Medical and Dental   _____

Mortgage or Rent   _____

Property Taxes   _____

Taxes   _____

  Federal   _____

  State   _____

  Social Security   _____

Utilities   _____

  Telephone   _____

  Gas, Electric, Water   _____

Other Expenses   _____

Total Expenses   _____

Monthly Income
Salary

  Yours   _____

  Spouse's   _____

Dividends   _____

Investment Income   _____

Other Income   _____

Total Income   _____

If you had more money, what would you do with it? Get out of debt? Take a trip or vacation? Move into a bigger house, have nicer furnishings, invest in art or antiques? Purchase a new car? Save for your retirement? College funds for your children? A rainy day? Go into business for yourself?

Consider the Importance of Time

How much time are you used to putting in every week? Would you like to work fewer hours while continuing to earn the same level of income? Are you finding you've spent so much time at the office that you don't have much of a personal or social life? Do you want more time for your family, your friends, and yourself? Would you be willing to take a position where you made less money but had more time?

If you had more time, what would you do with it? Play more golf or tennis? Spend your summer weekends on a sailboat? Take up a new hobby like painting or playing the piano? See more of your children or grandchildren? Travel across the United States, to Europe, Japan, or China, or take a cruise around the world?

Refine Your Lists
Go through the *Work I Enjoy* and *Things to Change* lists and narrow each list down to about seven items.

Figure Out What Motivates You

What makes you feel fulfilled, satisfied, or content? What gets you excited? What are your consuming passions? What brings peace and tranquillity to your life? What keeps you interested, alert, and on your toes? Do you enjoy competing with others, or do you prefer competing against your own best achievements? Do you constantly need new challenges? Do you enjoy the thrill of new ideas and concepts or the satisfaction of learning new skills? Do you usually reach for the next level, and push yourself even farther? Would you take additional courses or classes in order to further your career?

Have you ever considered a transitional move as a way of advancing your career? If you've been under a lot of stress perhaps you need a break. Would you consider looking for an interesting short-term position and plan to keep it for only a year or two? This might give you the opportunity to "recharge your batteries" and provide you with more time to plan your next career move. It could also be an opportunity to expand and develop some of the skills and talents you haven't used very often during your last job, to "apprentice" yourself in a new field you've been curious about, or to test the waters for starting your own business.

Recall Your Early Ambitions

Looking back a few years to high school or college, what did you dream of doing in the future? Which activities made you feel good and gave you confidence? What did you do well? What kinds of activities or organizations did you participate in? Student government? Clubs? Sports? Did you win any awards? What courses of study did you enjoy? What motivated you, and why? What were you curious about? Is there anything you wanted to do when you were younger that you still want to do now? Put your lists in a file labeled *Early Ambitions*.

Define Your Preferred Work Style

Do you prefer a more predictable, well-structured daily routine or are you more comfortable in a flexible, casual environment? Do you like to get to the office very early in the morning, before everybody else has arrived, stay late into the evening, or work from nine to five? Is your peak work time in the morning, afternoon, evening, or in the middle of the night? Do you prefer working near your home or is a longer commute OK? Would you rather talk to people on the telephone, meet with them face to face, or work on your own as much as possible? Do you make your best decisions independently or in group brainstorming sessions?

Refine Your Lists

Now go through the *Skills and Talents* and *Accomplishments* lists and shorten each to about seven items.

Through the process of setting your priorities, you've started to pinpoint the skills and individual qualities you have to offer an employer and identified the aspects of a job that are most important to you. These lists will become the basis of your resume, which you'll begin writing shortly. They'll help you prepare for your telephone conversations with potential employers. And you'll refer to them again when you begin the interviewing process and when you negotiate the terms of your employment.

Describe Yourself in Power Words

Make a list of words that describe you and the things you've done. Choose words with pizzazz, punch, and power.

Practice thinking about yourself in these terms, using words that have impact. Carry this list around with you. Review it over and over again. Pay attention to how you talk about yourself with other people, and start using these terms to describe yourself. Put a copy of your list in a file labeled *Words That Describe Me*.

This is a sample list of power words. You can certainly add more words.

ambitious	determined	motivator
assertive	direct	open-minded
authoritative	disciplined	optimistic
bright	dynamic	personable
broad-minded	energetic	practical
charming	enthusiastic	principled
compassionate	experienced	risk-taker
considerate	honest	self-confident
creative	innovative	self-determined
curious	insightful	straightforward
dedicated	intelligent	thorough
dependable	knowledgeable	trustworthy
detailed	leader	

Write a Story About Your Ideal Job

Write a story describing your new job and the contributions you'll make to your new company. What do you visualize your position to be? What types of responsibilities will you have on a daily basis? How will you spend a typical day at the office? What kinds of decisions will you be making? What impact will your presence have on the firm's profitability? What will your compensation package be? What will your office look like?

Practice reading your story out loud, to yourself, your family, and your friends. Pretend you're an actor on a stage, giving the performance of a lifetime. Learn to talk about yourself with conviction and enthusiasm, so that you'll convey the depth and substance that make you the person you are. Believe in yourself. This practice will be helpful for you when you begin to schedule your interviews with prospective employers. Put your story in a file labeled *My Ideal Job*.

Canvass Your Friends

You can get some innovative ideas for different types of careers by talking to your friends. Call your closest friends and schedule appointments with them for the specific purpose of asking what they see as your strongest skills and talents. What do they think you would be good at? What kind of work do they think you would most enjoy doing?

You'll probably feel embarrassed and a bit apprehensive when you make your first call, but you'll quickly discover that your friends will be more than happy to talk with you about your job search. Your ultimate objective is to meet with ten friends, but do it one at a time so you won't be overwhelmed. Don't attempt to schedule your next meeting until the previous one has taken place.

Bring an open mind, and just listen. You'll probably find that they come up with a lot of creative and interesting ideas, many of which you may never have considered. Take detailed notes of their comments. You may even want to record the conversations so you can play them back later and think about what was said. This will give you lots of food for thought.

Ask your friends how they think you should go about pursuing and following up on their ideas and suggestions. Who can they introduce you to? Could they set up any interviews for you?

Have any of your friends or business associates recently changed jobs themselves? Ask them how they did it. They may be able to give you some additional insights or suggestions based on their own recent experiences. Put your notes in a file labeled *My Friends' Ideas*.

5
Compose Your Resume

Its Purpose

You've now accumulated a great deal of information about yourself, but before you start writing your resume, think about its purpose. It will assist you in selling yourself to a potential employer by providing the most important and meaningful facts about your abilities, your experience, and the skills and talents you have to offer an organization.

Your printed resume is a written summary of your most outstanding accomplishments, a document you can leave behind after an interview or, if necessary, send out to somebody prior to scheduling an interview. (As I've said before, I think it's a waste of time to blindly send stacks of resumes. You could get lucky, of course, and land an interview or perhaps even a job offer. However, in today's highly competitive economic environment, the probability that you'll receive a job offer simply because you mailed out several hundred resumes isn't very high.)

Remember, you're trying to simplify the life of the person who's wading through a stack of resumes. The sooner somebody is hired, the sooner this busy manager can address the other projects that haven't been getting enough time and attention.

You want to write a resume that is easy to read and grabs the reader's attention. You want a potential employer to say, "This is an applicant I want to meet. This person sounds like someone who could help solve my problems, make my life easier, and help the firm make more money." A potential employer wants to see a resume that is short, crisp, and to the point. The shorter the better. Remember the advice offered by a well-dressed woman—put on *all* your jewelry, then begin to remove it, one piece at a time, until you have that *right* look. Do the same thing with your resume. When you're laying it out and designing it, remember: less is more. The more white space on the page, the better it looks, and it can only be *one* page in length.

Many people include in their resumes irrelevant details that fill up valuable space on the page. Unless this information is relevant to the job description, eliminate it and clean up your resume:

- Don't go to great lengths describing your goals, dreams, and objectives. An employer wants to know how your presence can help meet the company's goals and objectives.
- Don't merely talk about how you helped your company increase sales. Prospective employers will be much more inter-

ested in how you increased profits or improved profit margins.

- Don't use abbreviations. The person reading your resume may not know what they mean.
- Don't include information about your age, height, weight, health, or marital status. It isn't necessary.
- Don't write "References available upon request." This phrase is redundant and should be assumed.
- Don't list every position you've ever had, especially going back fifteen to twenty years. Don't list every city you've worked in.
- Don't go into great detail about where you went to school or what degrees you've earned unless you graduated very recently. Don't list college awards earned ten or fifteen years ago, grade point averages, or outside activities or hobbies.

Content and Meaning

You've now accumulated all the information you need to put your resume together. You've identified your skills and talents, itemized your accomplishments, and developed a long list of the many things you can offer a new employer. Pull out your various files and refresh your memory. Think of the major facts about yourself that you would want a future employer to know.

Make two new lists on separate pieces of paper. Label one *Accomplishments* and the other *Abilities*.

Review your *Work I Enjoy*, *Things to Change*, and *Accomplishments* lists. From these items, choose the ten or twelve things you've done that you think are the most important for a prospective employer to know about you and list them under *Accomplishments*.

Next, draw the ten or twelve key items from your *Skills and Talents*, *My Friends' Ideas*, and *Early Ambitions* lists and write them under *Abilities*. Notice these lists are so closely linked that several items could probably be entered on both lists. This is a very good sign—it shows that you've identified all the things you do well. Look through the other lists you've made for any additional items you would like to include under either *Accomplishments* or *Abilities*. Remember to describe your accomplishments and abilities in terms that show they can be easily utilized in many different businesses or industries. This affords you the opportunity to expand your career horizons.

Combine the two new lists onto a single page, placing what you feel is the most important information at the top. You'll probably rearrange this single list several times over the next few days. Don't expect to complete this in one sitting. Work on it a little bit at a time, and take time to think between sessions. Each time you return to it, you'll have a slightly better perception of the document you're creating.

Your objective is to be very specific and concise. Remove all unnecessary words. If you're using a computer or word processor, it will be easy to move things around. If you're writing longhand or using a typewriter, this will be a bit more time-consuming.

Now set aside the sheet of accomplishments and

abilities and start thinking about your future job description. What are you looking for in a job? Don't think in terms of a position title but in terms of daily activities or responsibilities. What do you see yourself doing every day? Review your *People I Admire* and *My Ideal Job* files as well as your earlier thinking about the value of time, money, and working environment.

Return to your resume draft and compile your employment history. You've stated your skills, talents, and accomplishments at the top of the page, where they will be most prominent to the reader. Place your employment history at the bottom of the page, listing the most recent job first. If you want to emphasize your past positions or titles to illustrate your record of promotions and increasing responsibility, for instance, lay out your employment history this way:

PQR Manufacturing	President	1990–Present
XYZ Manufacturing	Vice President	1987–1990
ABC Manufacturing	Sales Manager	1982–1987

(I've excluded the city and state so that the page looks neater and less cluttered.)

If you *don't* want to emphasize your past employment, perhaps because it includes a demotion, lay out your employment history this way:

PQR Manufacturing	Chicago, IL	1990–Present
XYZ Manufacturing	Chicago, IL	1987–1990
ABC Manufacturing	Chicago, IL	1982–1987

Don't bother to break down your employment

history by months. It really isn't important. Don't itemize every position or title you've had within an organization; it just makes your resume look cluttered. If you haven't got a great deal of experience, condense your work history at the bottom of the page where it's less prominent and expand your attention-getting list of accomplishments at the top.

When you describe your educational background, state the schools from which you received degrees, the degrees earned, and the year of graduation. Don't itemize every school you have ever attended. It isn't really important, particularly if you've been working for more than five years.

XYZ University	Master's in Business Administration	1985
ABC University	Bachelor's in Business Administration	1983

Place the most recent degree at the top of the list. Make sure that your tab settings line up with the other settings you've used elsewhere on the page.

Format and Layout

Your name, address, and telephone number should be centered at the top of the page, followed by the different sections of your resume—*Career Objective, Accomplishments, Abilities, Employment History*, and *Educational Background*—and the whole resume must fit on one typed page. If you can't squeeze it all onto one page at this point, do some additional rewriting until you can. Which words can be eliminated? Could several points be combined into one? Be even more specific, concise, and ruthless in your editing. Force yourself to focus on and pinpoint what you want to say about yourself.

Visual First Impressions

Your resume must make a great first impression—there won't be a second chance. Make it easy for people to learn about you. Starting with the first word of the first line, describe your skills, talents, and accomplishments in the most positive and flattering way you can. You're attempting to set a hook so that the people who read your resume will want to learn more about you and to meet you. Assume that readers will look at your resume for no more than fifteen seconds. If you haven't grabbed their attention by then, you're history!

Your resume must look neat and crisp and be free of spelling or typographical errors. There are many things you can do to make your resume stand out next to the hundreds of others that are received. Create a visually interesting document by experimenting with different layouts. With the powerful personal computers, sophisticated word processing programs, and laser printers available today, it's easy to make your resume look like a professionally typeset document. There are even inexpensive computer programs designed specifically to assist in writing resumes and cover letters.

Print your resume on a laser printer with scalable typefaces. A dot matrix printer will not give your resume a polished look, and anything typed on a regular typewriter looks unsophisticated these days. If you own a computer but not a laser printer, copy your resume on a disk and find somebody who can print it with a laser printer for you. If you don't own a computer, take your resume to a professional printing service.

Have your resume printed on white or ivory twenty- or twenty-four-pound cotton and linen paper. This will give it a professional look and feel. Print your cover letters on a laser printer if possible, and use stationery and envelopes that match your resume.

Let me define a few of the terms used to describe the appearance of text printed by a laser printer. A *typeface* is a family of letters, digits, and characters designed with a distinctive pattern. The term *font* refers to three elements: typeface (e.g., Times Roman or Helvetica), weight (e.g., bold or italic), and point size (e.g., 10-point or 12-point type. A point is 1/72 of an inch.) Here is an example of the Helvetica typeface, printed in four different weights and point sizes:

12-point Helvetica Roman

15-point Helvetica Italic

18-point Helvetica Bold

21-point Helvetica Bold Italic

The term *scalable font* or *scalable typeface* refers to the ability of the printer to change the size of the type; for example:

from extra large

to large

to small

to fine

When you start designing your resume, consider using a professional-looking typeface such as Times Roman for your regular text and Helvetica Bold for the headings (*Career Objectives*, *Educational Background*, etc.). Let's consider the resumes on pages 48–51 to see how to transform a basic resume into one that is visually interesting.

Resume One was typed using a Brougham typeface with 12cpi (characters per inch). Notice how cluttered the page looks. And it even has typographical errors. It's difficult for a reader to focus on the key points.

Resume Two has been edited, correcting spelling and punctuation errors, and laid out in a different manner. The career objective has been reworded in order to expand and highlight the transferability of the applicant's skills. It looks much cleaner, is easier to read, and makes a very favorable impression.

Resume Three was printed on a laser printer using Times Roman as the typeface for the text and Helvetica Bold for the headings. The asterisks (*) were replaced by squares (■). Bullets (•) could also have been used. As you can see, there is a world of difference between a typewriter and a laser printer. This resume looks great!

Cover Letters

A resume that will be mailed to a prospective employer must be accompanied by a cover letter. The cover letter should be straightforward and brief, and you must be especially careful to spell the person's name correctly. The cover letter should not repeat all the information contained in your resume. State the

STEPHEN S. STRICKLAND
1201 N. Highland Drive
Bloomington, Il. 61701
309/824-7692

OBJECTIVE: Senior executive position overseeing sales, marketing and
administration with construction/manufacturing company

EMPLOYMENT HISTORY:

4/88 -   **TRYTEX CORP.**
present   **Executive Vice President** - operations
                * negotiated purchase of phone system reducing costs 41%
                * designed and created employee training program which
                  increased productivity and reduced absenteeism by 18%
                * instituted program which reduced accidents by 45%
                * Devoleped procedures improving plant effeciency 16%

6/86-2/88   **FLOYD SMITH COMPANY**
                Field Superintendent
                * Mystec Corporate Headquarters - field superintendent on
                  $13 million project, was on schedule and under budget
                * supervised field personnel on projects of $15 million,
                  produced weekly reports of materials used

8/80 - 4/86   **SOUTHWIND DEVELOPMENT COMPANY**
                Project Manager & Estimator - commercial office buildings,
                  industrial buildings and residintial complexes
                * managed construction of projects of over $10 million
                * wrote feasibility studies for new biulding construction

3/76 - 4/80   **STRICKLAND & ASSOCIATES, INC.**
                Consultant
                * developed a computerized billing and production system
                * designed and developed Quality Assurance programs

1965-1975   **LOMBARDI BROTHERS, INC.**
                President and General Manager
                * joined family manufacturing company after college;
                  positions included plant manager, purchasing agent,
                  sales director and president. Company was sold in 1975

EDUCATION: NORTHERN UNIVERSITY, Des Moines, Iowa Graduated 1965
                B.S. in Business Administration; minor in Economics

CIVIC: SOUTH SHORE HOSPITAL BOARD
                Eight years on Board of Bloomington National Bank; six
                years as president of the Park District; treasurer of
                local chapter of United Way; Northern Alunmi Varsity Club

Resume One

STEPHEN S. STRICKLAND
1201 N. Highland Drive
Bloomington, IL. 61701
309 824-7692

OBJECTIVE   Senior management position with daily responsibilities
within corporate administration, sales, or marketing

ABILITIES

* Developed computerized billing and production
  scheduling system, increasing productivity
* Wrote feasibility studies for the construction
  of warehouse, office, and manufacturing facilities
* Created quality assurance programs, reducing costs
* Instituted safety programs, reducing accidents by 45 percent
* Supervised construction personnel on jobs of up to $15,000,000

ACHIEVEMENTS

* Completed $13,000,000 project on schedule and under budget
* Developed training program, reducing absenteeism by 18 percent
* President of manufacturing company. Previous positions included
  plant manager, purchasing agent, sales & marketing director
* Negotiated purchase of phone system, reducing costs by 41 percent
* Developed new plant procedures, improving efficiency by 16 percent
* President of South Shore Hospital Board, Director of Bloomington
  National Bank, President of Park District, Treasurer of United Way

EMPLOYERS

Trytex Corp. - Executive Vice President   1988 - Present
Floyd Smith Company - Field Superintendent   1986 - 1988
Southwind Development Co. - Project Manager   1980 - 1986
Strickland & Associates, Inc. - Consultant   1976 - 1980
Lombardi Brothers, Inc. - President   1965 - 1975

EDUCATION

Northern University, Des Moines, Iowa - Graduated 1965

Resume Two

STEPHEN S. STRICKLAND
1201 N. Highland Drive
Bloomington, IL. 61701
309 824-7692

OBJECTIVE   Senior management position with daily responsibilities
within corporate administration, sales, or marketing

ABILITIES

* Developed computerized billing and production
  scheduling system, increasing productivity
* Wrote feasibility studies for the construction
  of warehouse, office, and manufacturing facilities
* Created quality assurance programs, reducing costs
* Instituted safety programs, reducing accidents by 45 percent
* Supervised construction personnel on jobs of up to $15,000,000

ACHIEVEMENTS

* Completed $13,000,000 project on schedule and under budget
* Developed training program, reducing absenteeism by 18 percent
* President of manufacturing company. Previous positions included
  plant manager, purchasing agent, sales & marketing director
* Negotiated purchase of phone system, reducing costs by 41 percent
* Developed new plant procedures, improving efficiency by 16 percent
* President of South Shore Hospital Board, Director of Bloomington
  National Bank, President of Park District, Treasurer of United Way

EMPLOYERS

Trytex Corp. - Executive Vice President   1988 - Present
Floyd Smith Company - Field Superintendent   1986 - 1988
Southwind Development Co. - Project Manager   1980 - 1986
Strickland & Associates, Inc. - Consultant   1976 - 1980
Lombardi Brothers, Inc. - President   1965 - 1975

EDUCATION

Northern University, Des Moines, Iowa - Graduated 1965

Resume Two

STEPHEN S. STRICKLAND
1201 North Highland Drive
Bloomington, Illinois 61701
309 824-7692

OBJECTIVE   Senior management position with daily responsibilities
within corporate administration, sales, or marketing

ABILITIES

- Developed computerized billing and production
  scheduling system, increasing productivity
- Wrote feasibility studies for the construction
  of warehouse, office, and manufacturing facilities
- Created quality assurance programs, reducing costs
- Instituted safety programs, reducing accidents by 45 percent
- Supervised construction personnel on jobs of up to $15,000,000

ACHIEVEMENTS

- Completed $13,000,000 project on schedule and under budget
- Developed training program, reducing absenteeism by 18 percent
- President of manufacturing company. Previous positions included
  plant manager, purchasing agent, sales & marketing director
- Negotiated purchase of phone system, reducing costs by 41 percent
- Developed new plant procedures, improving efficiency by 16 percent
- President of South Shore Hospital Board, Director of Bloomington
  National Bank, President of Park District, Treasurer of United Way

EMPLOYERS

Trytex Corp. - Executive Vice President	1988 - Present
Floyd Smith Company - Field Superintendent	1986 - 1988
Southwind Development Co. - Project Manager	1980 - 1986
Strickland & Associates, Inc. - Consultant	1976 - 1980
Lombardi Brothers, Inc. - President	1965 - 1975

EDUCATION

Northern University, Des Moines, Iowa - Graduated 1965

Resume Three

specific position you are interested in and how you learned of the opening, briefly discuss your experience, and refer the reader to the enclosed resume. At the end of the letter, indicate that you will telephone the prospective employer to schedule an interview.

You will need to write a separate cover letter for each position you apply for. Remember that the cover letter serves as your introduction to a prospective employer and that first impressions are important. Be sure your spelling and grammar are absolutely correct.

These are some things you should not do with your cover letter:

- Don't start your phrases with the word *I*. Whenever possible, begin a sentence with the word *you*, which has a much more powerful psychological appeal to the reader.
- Don't ask the prospective employer to call you to set up a meeting. It's *your* responsibility to follow up.
- Don't write flowery phrases that make little sense or could be interpreted as insulting to the recipient's intelligence or ego, especially if you're writing to the president or owner of the company. For example, "extensive experience with sophisticated, systems-oriented product lines, international business development, marketing, and operations" doesn't really mean anything. Use words and phrases that are part of your everyday language.

- Don't state your salary or compensation needs, even if the advertisement to which you're responding says to do so. Your purpose in writing is to let a potential employer know you're available and that your skills, talents, and experience will add value to the organization. You don't want to risk being passed over at this stage because your compensation goal is too high or too modest. (Salary negotiations will be discussed later.)
- Don't send photographs of yourself. Your looks have nothing to do with your qualifications for the job.
- Don't send photocopies of your resume.
- Don't have a secretary or assistant sign your cover letter for you.

Assemble a Marketing Package

There might be additional kinds of written information you could leave behind after an interview to help you sell yourself and show that you're thorough and detailed. For example, include copies of letters of recommendation, awards and citations you may have earned, or certificates of completion from professional seminars or outside courses you've taken. Also include any articles that you have written or were written about you or significant projects you worked on that have appeared in newspapers or magazines.

Don't just photocopy an article as it appeared in the newspaper or magazine. Create your own special layout instead. Cut out the name of the newspaper or magazine and center it with tape at the top of a piece of white paper. Center the article underneath the publication name, and leave margin space at the top and bottom and left and right sides of the page. Now make clean copies of the article. Under special circumstances, you may want to include the original article or the entire magazine (if you have some extra copies or back issues) as part of your marketing package. This makes an extremely favorable impression and sets you apart from the crowd.

6
Find People Who Can Offer You a Job

Expand Your Horizons

You now know the most marketable skills and talents you have to offer a company. You've pinpointed your abilities and achievements. Now you want to contact the greatest number of people possible—play the numbers game. You're looking for a job you'll find interesting, challenging, and financially rewarding. Give a lot of different people the opportunity to think about how your training and experience can help their firm solve its business problems and make more money.

For instance, let's say you enjoyed writing policy and procedure manuals at your old job with a large automobile dealership. Instead of considering your skills as limited to the automobile business, realize they're really associated with creating and writing manuals. Now how many industries need good people

55

who can do this? You've got health-care and insurance companies, restaurant chains, real-estate firms—the list is probably endless. There are certainly many companies who need to create this type of manual.

You want to expand your job search outside of the businesses or industries with which you're familiar. Be open-minded about what type of work you'll do and what type of industry you'll join. Don't get hung up on how newspapers, magazines, or investment analysts view an industry. They frequently use phrases like mature industry, on the leading edge, high technology, low technology, global industry, broad focus versus narrow focus. These categories really don't mean anything in terms of your potential for career satisfaction and advancement within a field. What's most important is the heart of the organization—the people you will work with and how you will fit in.

Don't be overly concerned if you're not familiar with the specific terms, phrases, or inner workings of an employer with whom you're trying to get an interview. New employees aren't expected to know everything. It's understood that it will take time to learn your responsibilities and duties once you start working there.

And don't lose sleep over your competition. There's nothing you can do about the other people applying for the same position. The only thing you can do is sell yourself—your previous training, education, and work experience—and convince the person who is interviewing you that you're capable of making wonderful contributions to the firm.

Know Who to Look For

Your objective is to meet people who can either offer you a job or introduce you to someone who can. Target your search aggressively. The large majority of available jobs are never advertised—the positions are filled either by word of mouth or by referral. To give yourself the opportunity to be in the right place at the right time, meet with and talk to as many people as possible.

Use Your Connections

Take advantage of all your connections and contacts. You've met hundreds of people throughout your career who may be in a position to help you by introducing you to the right people or, at the very least, offering encouragement. Be bold and contact everybody. Market the product you know best: yourself. Start telling everybody how good you are and about your wonderful skills and talents. Toot your own horn as often as you can to as many people as you can. The self-evaluation you've been working on for the past few days and weeks has been preparing you for this moment. You now know what to say and how to present yourself properly.

To find that pot of gold at the end of the rainbow, you'll have to contact a lot of people. If you come up with a list of only ten, twenty, or thirty potential contacts, you'll be out of names and options in just a matter of days. Expand your horizons and try to create a universe of potential names that numbers two hundred, three hundred, or even five hundred people.

As you become even more creative in your thinking and resourceful in your prospecting, you won't ever find yourself at a dead end because you will always have more alternatives.

Network, Network, Network

Create a prospect list of people to call and write their names on index cards, one name to a card. I will explain how to use your prospect cards a little later. You have two objectives when you talk with these people:

- To see if there are any employment opportunities within their organizations
- To see if they know any people who might be interested in meeting you

Let me first share some ideas about how to find people, and then I'll explain how to contact them.

You may have difficulty starting your prospect list, so begin with the easiest people you can think of: family members. Include your parents, brothers and sisters, cousins, aunts and uncles, and your in-laws. They may provide you with a large number of additional names.

Sit down with them and explore their network of contacts. Who do they know that you could be talking with? Do they know people who recently went into business for themselves? Got promoted? Changed jobs? How could your skills and talents be of benefit to those people?

Next, add your lawyer, banker, and accountant to your prospect list. They may be able to give you the names of some of their clients, associates, or colleagues to contact. Are there other people within their organizations you've talked with in the past? How about the lawyers, bankers, and accountants of your friends and relatives?

Contact your former coworkers or colleagues for contacts they could provide you with. Who were you friendly with? Who did you know casually? Who are the people you previously worked with who have gone into other businesses, industries, or professions? They may have discovered fascinating new careers you should know about. You may have good relationships with some of your former customers, clients, or vendors. Share your situation with them and see what suggestions they come up with.

Quite often your friends and contacts within an industry can help you find a new job. Someone you know may have changed firms and be aware of an opening there that you could fill. If you've let that person know you're looking for new career opportunities, he or she may give you a call and tip you off about the opening.

If you need more names, let your mind wander. Contact everybody you've had a business relationship with, and anyone else who comes to mind. What about your former competitors in business? Don't leave any stone unturned.

Your nonbusiness relationships can also generate kickoffs for business opportunities. Who are the people who have interests and hobbies similar to yours? Who are the people you've gravitated to and developed long-term friendships and relationships with? These are the people you may find yourself going into business with in the future. Talk with people who are members of the same organizations or clubs you belong to. If you have access to membership lists or telephone directories, try contacting some of these people. People you know casually may be in a position to introduce you to their associates.

Don't forget your Rolodex, your address book, and that pile of business cards you've collected over the years, which you either copied before you left your last position or which your former employer permitted you to take with you. There may be hundreds of names in there. Every business is looking for experienced, talented, and hardworking people who can add value to their organization.

Tap into Organizations

In addition to using your network of friends, relatives, and associates, take advantage of group meetings where you can talk with many people at a luncheon or over cocktails. Your local newspaper probably prints a weekly listing of scheduled business meetings or seminars. The Chamber of Commerce has regular monthly meetings, and, in addition, they may sponsor meetings on specific business topics or related subjects. Get on the mailing list. Make it a practice to attend at least one or two meetings each week. Don't be in a hurry to spend money to join these organizations, but do try to attend as a guest. If possible, get a copy of the membership directory or a list of the current officers and directors. You'll have more people to contact.

Keep Your Eyes and Ears Open

When you're talking to people, ask them questions about what they do, their company, their industry, what they like and don't like about their specific business. Be a good listener, and try to obtain as much information as you possibly can about them. Don't be in a hurry to tell them your life story. You'll have the opportunity to do that later. You just want to meet them under the most favorable conditions. You're trying to obtain more names, telephone numbers, and information. Spend your time with people who are in a position to hire you or introduce or refer you to those who are. Don't waste your time with other people who are looking for work. That won't get you a job.

When you meet prospects, always ask for their business cards, and be sure to leave your own name and telephone number, so when you contact them they'll remember who you are and where you met.

Have your own business cards printed, even if you're not presently working. The card alone may open up conversations for you. When you give out a business card that doesn't have a company name or title on it, people will probably ask what kind of work you do. Then you have the perfect opening to explain how you're exploring new business opportunities. If you don't have a business card with you at the time, ask people to write your name on the back of one of theirs. The chance that they'll remember you is much greater if they write your name instead of you writing it for them.

Follow Up Immediately

After meeting new people, contact them the following day by phone and tell them how much you enjoyed meeting them. State that you thought their business

sounded very interesting. Ask if you could come in
and talk with them for half an hour to learn more
about what they do. These will be exploratory meetings, where you'll do more fact-finding about who
these people are, and what they, their companies, and
their industries do. You're not looking for a job at this
point. You're exploring.

What do people like and dislike about their jobs?
Where do they see their careers going? How did they
get into their line of work? What specific skills and
talents are needed for this business? What are the
opportunities for career advancement? How is the
industry doing? Who are their major competitors?
(With the names of their competitors, you've obtained
more people to call.)

Explain why you're interested in what they're
doing. What do you find fascinating about their
work? How do you see yourself contributing to an
organization?

Using the telephone to follow up instead of sending letters maintains your excitement, enthusiasm,
and that sense of urgency you may need to keep
going. Time is of the essence. When you send a letter,
you typically wait several days before following up,
assuming the letter went out promptly. After a few
days have passed, there's the chance you may forget,
or find a convenient excuse for not making the call,
often due to a fear of being rejected.

Meet people at their place of business. This way
you'll have the opportunity to see what their offices
look like. Don't meet over lunch, even if someone else
is buying. You're looking for a new career and want
this serious business meeting to take place without
interruptions or distractions.

As you talk to other people, you'll discover that they aren't nearly as intimidating as you might have feared. They each have two eyes, two ears, a nose, and a mouth. What you will learn is that these people found something they enjoyed doing, and they were able to turn that interest or hobby into a business or career.

Always Wear Your Prospecting Cap

When you go to somebody's office, look at the mailing labels on the magazines in the reception area. They may identify the senior executives or principals of the firm. While you're waiting, study the trade journals on the coffee table. There could be a wealth of information inside. If they seem to be of interest, ask the receptionist if it would be all right to take one of the older issues so you can study it in more detail at home. If the answer is no, take down the name and phone number of the publisher, and when you get home, call and ask for several back issues and subscription information. You may choose not to subscribe, but will certainly gain access to more names.

Look through the magazines for interesting companies or people. Study the advertisements. Jot the names on prospect cards, call each company that appears interesting, and ask for additional information. Who are the columnists? Who wrote the letters to the editor? In addition, contact the editors or publishers. They could possibly have a few leads for you.

If the person you're meeting works in an office building, study the building's directory. Are there any other businesses listed on the directory that you think may be of interest? More names.

Generate Leads from Newspapers, Magazines, and Trade Journals

As you can see, it's relatively easy to come up with lots of names of people to contact. Turn your people search into a game, have some fun, and challenge yourself. Try to find five, ten, fifteen people a day. There are many companies that are doing interesting and creative things, and all it takes is a bit of detective work on your part to find them.

Here are some more ideas. Start with your local newspapers. Study the business section every day. Look for the names of people who have been promoted or who have changed jobs. Call their employers. They could be hiring. Who just landed a new account or closed a big contract? Has a company had a change in top management? There may be openings because a new president will want to bring in a new staff. Who was profiled on the front page? Study the entire paper. Look for the names of companies that are doing something worth being written about. Which companies are spending money on advertisements? More potential prospects.

Many cities have local business journals, issued on a weekly or monthly basis. There are also trade journals and industry publications that serve specific, targeted audiences. Subscribe to those that interest you or review them regularly at your local library. Study the national business magazines such as *Business Week*, *Forbes*, and *Fortune*, searching for more people or businesses who are doing something. You can even look through the yellow pages for leads.

When you locate companies or individuals you think would be worth contacting, write their names on prospect cards and start calling, one person at a time.

All Prospects Are Not Created Equal

I realize that some of these people will probably have considerably more potential than others, but don't expect your rate of success for scheduling appointments with any of them to be better than 10 percent. This means that if you attempt to contact one hundred individuals, you can consider yourself very successful if you actually meet with ten of them. Of these ten meetings, six or seven won't produce any tangible results. But it will be good practice, and you give yourself the opportunity to talk with and meet new people. There will be three or four people who will hold some promise.

This is indeed a shotgun approach. By the time you find the job you're looking for, you may easily have contacted three, four, or even five hundred people. But by continuing to search for people to talk with about job opportunities, eventually you'll be in the right place with the right person who will appreciate and understand how your skills, talents, energy, and enthusiasm will make his or her organization even better.

You'll greatly improve your chances of finding the job you want simply because you take the time to *ask* for an interview. You may even meet someone who will create a job just for you, because the firm is growing and your skills and talents will clearly add value to the organization by helping them solve a problem. There's an appropriate old saying: "The harder I work, the luckier I get."

Look at all of your interview opportunities as if you were a batter in a baseball game. There are two ways to strike out: you can go down swinging, or you can take a called third strike. In the latter case, the batter watches the ball but doesn't swing. By just waiting for something to happen, the batter is not participating. Then there is the aggressive hitter who swings at the good pitches and takes every opportunity to try to hit them. Even when swinging and missing, the batter is still trying, and if the batter hits the ball directly at someone, there's always the possibility that the ball will roll through the fielder's legs or be dropped or thrown away. If you're not actively swinging, your chances of getting on base aren't very good.

Throughout my life, I've found that people who struggle day after day and don't give up eventually succeed. Of course there are road blocks, stumbling blocks, barricades, and dead ends. But that's all part of life. When you feel tired and run down, take a break, recharge your batteries, get a good night's sleep, and start over in the morning.

Pinpoint an Industry

If, after you've talked with a number of people, you've pinpointed an industry you think is especially interesting, do some additional research. Go to the public library and talk to the business librarian. Stop by the placement office at your local college or university or visit the local office of the State Department of Labor. They have a wealth of valuable and meaningful information, resources that are often overlooked.

This will give you the opportunity to discover

which companies are in the business and who the major players are. This kind of information is also published regularly in the major business magazines, which produce industry-specific lists, providing a great deal of information and sometimes including addresses and telephone numbers.

When you do your research, copy the important information from the reference material so you can read and study it on your own. Call these companies and ask them to send you information about themselves and their services or products. Try to get financial information like annual reports or proxy statements if they're available. In addition to the financial information, annual reports provide the names of all corporate officers and directors as well as listing subsidiaries and their locations. These individuals could all become people for you to contact in your job search. The annual report can also tip you off to the financial health of a company. If it's been having troubles, it may not be an organization with which you would want to become involved. If the company is private and annual reports aren't available, ask for copies of the sales literature, catalogs, or brochures. Perhaps you could obtain a list of the officers and find out their job responsibilities. Learn as much as you can about these companies.

Consider contacting more than one person within an organization. Different departments within a company may not communicate with each other about their need to fill an open position, so one department may not have any openings while another is looking for several people. In addition, ask for the name of the person who heads human resources or the personnel department and contact him or her. In a well-run company, this person knows the current staffing needs of the whole organization and tries to keep in touch with qualified applicants should a position become available. With this approach, you're covering all your bases.

When you target a specific industry, you may discover there are not many potential employers located where you're presently living. If this is the case, you'll be forced to communicate with these companies by the telephone and through the mail. When the conversations become more serious they'll probably invite you to come to their offices for interviews; and should they offer you a job, expect to move to another city.

If there are enough potential companies in another city, such as New York, Los Angeles, or Chicago, you may want to take a hotel room for a week or two and schedule interviews while you're in town. You could also try to line up interviews for a specific date in the future, and plan to come into the city for a day or two.

Decide How You'd Feel About Relocating

If you've decided to pursue a specific business or industry out of town, give yourself enough time to sort out your feelings about relocating to a new city. There are many things to consider before you make up your mind to move. Where are you coming from, and where would you be moving to? If you're familiar with big-city life, would you enjoy living in a smaller town? If you're from the East Coast, would you like the Midwest, or vice versa? What would you do if you took a job in a new city and then found that you or your family didn't like living there? What would you do if you took the job, moved, and shortly thereafter lost your job due to unforeseen economic circumstances?

How happy will your spouse and children be? If your spouse is working, how easy will it be for him or her to find a new position? How would your children like this new community? How good is the school system? If your family didn't move, how comfortable would you be commuting between your home and your job?

How will you go about addressing your housing needs? How much money will it cost if you'll be moving from a real-estate market that is soft to a city where the market is hot? A recent newspaper article told the story of an executive who moved from Dallas to New Jersey, where he purchased a $350,000 home. Three years later he relocated to Chicago, but because the housing market had collapsed, he only received $270,000 for his New Jersey home. Is it possible that you could end up owning two houses at the same time? What would you do then?

These are questions that require a great deal of thought and consideration on your part. A mistake could cost you a lot of money.

Read the Want Ads . . . If You Insist

As you know, I believe the odds of finding a job through the want ads are rather slim. It can be a time-consuming, tedious, and overwhelming process. There are so many ads to look at, it'll make your head spin. But if you want to give it a try, these tips will make your life a bit easier.

Give yourself plenty of time to absorb all the information you're reading, and allow yourself at least thirty to sixty minutes, without interruptions, to study the newspaper. Do this on a daily basis, first thing in the morning while the advertisements are fresh. Time is of the essence. If you wait a few days, or even hours, the ads become stale, since everybody else has already had the opportunity to respond to them. On Saturday afternoon, get the Sunday newspaper and pick out the ads that excite you, so you can be the first person to call on Monday morning.

When you're looking at a full page of ads, you may find it easier to read the ads from left to right, instead of top to bottom.

- Take a piece of white paper and place it beneath the ad you're looking at. This keeps your eyes focused.
- Skim the ad quickly, and if you think it's worth studying in more detail, circle it with a red pen.
- If it doesn't interest or excite you, put an X through the ad.
- Work your way across the page, return to the left edge, and skim the next row.
- After you've completed your review of the entire paper, go back and read the ads you circled more thoroughly. Cut out the ads you think are promising, and throw out the remainder of the paper.
- Tape each ad to a prospect (index) card so you'll be able to process them quickly and efficiently. Then you'll have an opportunity to write your thoughts and comments on the cards.

- Go through your collection of ads, and decide in which order they should be called.

If the ad asks you to send your resume, call anyway. Try to get the name of the person who is doing the interviewing for this job, or ask for the president. If the ad gives only a post office box, without a company name and address, you're probably wasting your time by responding. You haven't got the slightest idea to whom you're writing. You're blindly throwing darts at a target and praying. Don't be in a hurry to send your resume in the mail. If you do, you'll become one of a cast of thousands, which is the situation you're trying to avoid.

Plan to get on the telephone at 8:00 A.M. every morning, especially on Monday mornings. Be the first person to call in response to the ad. If the person you need to speak with is tied up, find out when he or she will be available. If you talk to a secretary or assistant, attempt to learn as much about the position as possible. Don't leave a message asking that your call be returned. It probably won't be. It's your responsibility to get through.

7
Setting Up Interviews

Work Your Prospect Cards

The best way to keep track of all the people you're trying to reach is by creating a prospect card system using index cards. Index cards come in several sizes. If you're able to write small, you may prefer a 3″ × 5″ card. If you like a lot of space, try the larger ones. When you're trying to contact and keep in touch with large numbers of people, index cards provide you with much more flexibility than a pad of paper with a list of twenty-five names written on it. Because you write only one name on each card, this system allows you to easily separate the people you wish to keep in touch with from those you don't plan to contact again. You can now stay in touch with hundreds of people, and keep track of where you stand with each and every one of them.

These cards become a case history or diary, your written record of all your conversations, meetings, and discussions. Keep as much information as possible on the front of each card. Don't write on the back—you may not remember to turn it over. If you find you need a second card, tape it over the front of the first card, and rewrite the name and telephone number. Whenever you have a conversation with that person, write the date at the left edge and right next to it the event that took place: a meeting, telephone call, etc. Then record what will happen next.

- Will you be calling or writing next?
- Will the person be sending you information?
- When should you follow up?
- Will that person call you, or should you call first?

Write neatly and don't skip spaces. Go ahead and use abbreviations in your notes to yourself in order to save space. Jot down the names of the receptionist and secretaries directly under the telephone number so that when you call you can refer to them by name. (It makes a very favorable impression.)

These cards will help you remember the specific conversations you've had with many people because you're relying on your notes, not your memory. If there is any work you need to do, follow up on, or keep track of, make a notation on your Master List as well. This way you won't forget about any unfinished work. Make it a habit to refresh your memory before any telephone conversations or meetings by reviewing your cards and notations.

When you obtain someone's business card, tape it to the upper left-hand corner of a prospect card. Don't staple the cards because then they won't lay flat. If you will be handling a lot of business cards, you'll probably prefer to work with the larger index cards. Just below the business card write the date and place where you met or how the card was obtained.

If you find a name from a newspaper, magazine, or referral, write it in the upper left-hand corner using a pen (pencils smudge and soon become illegible). Don't waste your time trying to type prospect cards. Write the phone number in the upper right-hand corner where it will be easy to see. While you're accumulating your cards, just write the name if that's all you have at the moment. Go back later and add the address and telephone number when you get that information.

943-0763

JOEL SMITH   SEC:RHONDA
SMITH & GREY ADVERTISING RECP'T: BEVERLY
101 E. WACKER DRIVE
CHICAGO

4/15 – MET AT C.A.C.I. LUNCHEON
        – CHATTED BRIEFLY. VERY FRIENDLY.
4/16 – SEC: RHONDA – OUT ALL DAY. TRY 4/18 IN P.M.
4/18 – VERY FRIENDLY. TRAVELING 'TILL 5/1. CALL 5/3
5/3 – RHONDA: MEETING ALL A.M. TRY AFTER 2:00 P.M.
5/3 – APPOINTMENT 5/7 2:00 THERE.
5/7 – APP'T CHANGED TO 5/9 10:00 A.M.

Organize by Date

Keep prospect cards in a card box, and use dividers numbered 1 to 31 to keep track of the people you're trying to reach. Rotate the numbered cards forward each day of the month so that the current day is always at the front of the box, and yesterday's numbered card is placed at the back, behind all the others. Tomorrow's prospect cards will always be next in line.

For example, you call a prospect, and the secretary tells you that the person will be out of town until next Monday, the twenty-first of the month. You decide that it would be best to call on Tuesday. Jot your brief notes on the prospect card and place it behind the divider card tabbed 22. When the twenty-second comes, the card is right there waiting for you.

When you're ready to make your calls, take the cards behind the divider with today's date, put the stack in front of you, and start dialing (placing today's divider card at the back of the box). Now the divider with tomorrow's date has moved to the front of the box. Your divider cards continue to move forward. This is a much simpler method of keeping track of the people you want to call than grouping all your cards together with a rubber band. If, at the end of your phoning session, there are people you didn't reach, replace those cards behind tomorrow's divider card.

Using Your Cards

Pay close attention to how people talk to you on the telephone. Sometimes it can be a good indication as to how well or poorly the organization is doing. If everybody you speak with is friendly and polite, and you detect smiles in their voices, then the company is probably doing well. If people seem to be short with you, or are rude when you call, the company may be having problems.

Or it may be an indication that their business personality and yours aren't a good fit. Should this be the case, keep a wary eye open during all your discussions and conversations with the people at this company, for you may quickly come to the conclusion that this isn't the right place for you. Don't second-guess your gut reactions. If you're feeling something inside, explore it further, or just walk away from the situation before you get too involved. When you talk with somebody who isn't helpful or is unable to be of any assistance, throw away that prospect card. Sometimes simply throwing it away isn't gratifying enough; if it will make you feel better, rip it into little pieces first and then throw it away.

Keep notes on how easy people are to reach by phone. Some people are almost never available. They spend so much time in meetings, on the telephone, or out of the office that it's impossible to speak to them. They also aren't very likely to return your phone calls. Keep track of each attempt to reach them, the date, and the time of day you called. You may want to see if you can get through at 7:00 A.M. or 6:30 P.M. If you've tried at least six or seven times over a period of several weeks and have been unable to reach them, they're not worth pursuing any longer. It's time to move on. No matter who these people are, if it is impossible to have a conversation with them, then they aren't good prospects. If you continue to try to reach them, you'll end up wasting a lot of valuable time and energy.

Keeping Correspondence Files

When you start sending out correspondence, set up a generic file as a temporary place to hold copies of your letters and label it *Correspondence*. Include a brief note to yourself on each letter listing any enclosures, so you'll remember what was sent. When your conversations begin to get more serious, set up a separate file for each company.

Continue to keep notes and comments on all your communications and conversations with everybody you talk to. If you're still in preliminary discussions, jot your notes down right on the prospect card. If you already have a file for this company, create a *Case History Sheet* on a big piece of paper and leave it on the very top of the correspondence inside the folder. This will serve the same purpose as the prospect card, except that it's bigger and will stay right in your file. In the left margin, note the date whenever something happens—a telephone call, a letter, or anything else. Clip your prospect card to the *Case History Sheet*. Use both your Master List and your calendar to stay on top of any unfinished work.

Make the Telephone Your Friend

The fastest and most efficient way to reach anyone is by picking up the telephone. But you must be persistent. In today's fast-paced and hectic business world, it isn't easy to get through on the telephone. Most busy people are often in meetings, out of the office, or on the telephone themselves, so you may try five times on the average before you're able to get through. If you call only once or twice, you aren't giving yourself enough opportunities.

Let me explain. Suppose you had a list of one hundred people and called everybody on the list once. You would find that you had spoken to about twenty-five people. That leaves you with seventy-five you haven't reached. You call everyone in this group a second time, and you're able to speak to another twenty people. Now you've spoken to forty-five people, and you're left with fifty-five you haven't yet reached. As you try to reach the remaining people, it becomes more difficult. You'll find you're able to reach a handful when you call the third time, fewer the fourth time, and so on. But it becomes much harder, because the remaining people are the ones who just aren't available.

After you've tried to reach a person six or seven times, it's time to throw the name away and replace it with a fresh one. You'll find it's calling new people that gets you excited. You won't have much enthusiasm when you try to reach somebody who wasn't available the first six times you called. You can be pretty sure that that person won't be available on the seventh try either. And if you do finally get through on the phone, you'll discover that he or she hasn't got the time to talk with you.

Make the telephone your friend because it saves you time. Use it instead of the postal service. As you continually add names to your list of people to call, you're really looking for the ones who are available on the first, second, or third try. These people will become your best leads for getting a job.

Prepare for Your Calls

Whenever you're telephoning, assume the person you're calling will actually pick up the telephone, and be fully prepared to give your speech immediately. Make an outline of all the things you want to say. If it's helpful, write it out word for word and rehearse it before you make the call, but try not to read it over the phone—you'll sound unnaturally stiff and won't be yourself. To reduce some of the tension in your body and the fear in your heart, take a few deep breaths, sigh a few times, and try to relax. Tape the word *smile* in front of you. It'll help remind you to look forward to talking with and meeting these people, one of whom will become your new boss. It'll take some of the nervous edge off your voice.

The first few times you pick up the telephone, you'll probably be scared to death, but don't let that stop you. Build your confidence slowly. Try calling some of the easier people first—people you already know or people to whom you have an introduction. From them you would expect to receive a warmer response. Then become a bit braver and call the people you don't know. The worst thing that can happen is someone will hang up the phone. If you find yourself getting angry or frustrated, take a break. Get a cup of coffee or a soda, and give yourself a few minutes to calm down.

The best time to get on the telephone is first thing in the morning. Start "dialing for dollars" at 9:00 A.M. or earlier, and continue until 10:30 or 11:00. That's the time of day when you're most likely to catch businesspeople in their offices. It's also the time when you have the most energy and enthusiasm in your voice.

The next best time to call is between 2:30 and 4:30 in the afternoon.

Expect Rejection

Sure you're going to be rejected. So what else is new? Wouldn't you be surprised if everybody wanted to hire you? Your purpose in calling is to get an appointment, and when you use the telephone, you get answers quickly. You'll find some people won't even take your call; others will talk with you but won't set up an appointment; some will meet you but won't have any positions available. Because you persist you will eventually call someone who has a position available, wants to meet you, and schedules an interview, which just might lead to a job offer. But to succeed you've got to be aggressive and assertive, and you've got to sell yourself. Practice. Practice. Practice! If you're not being rejected, you're not trying hard enough.

Your bruised ego will heal rather quickly. Once you've gone through the experience of having people tell you no a few times, you'll realize it isn't so bad. Don't take these rejections personally. They have nothing to do with you. That idea alone should make you feel better. The majority of people you talk with will be courteous and friendly. Occasionally you'll speak with somebody who is angry, rude, or obnoxious. Get off the phone as quickly as possible, and be happy you don't work there.

How to Spot a Time Waster

When you speak with people on the phone, the first indication of how interested they are will be heard in their tone of voice and the length of time they spend talking to you. It won't take you long to discover that some people are sincere while others couldn't care less if they're wasting your time or their own.

With practice you'll learn how to feel people out. Some will tell you right off the bat that they're not interested and end the conversation abruptly. Your feelings will be hurt by their bluntness, but these people are actually doing you a favor and you should appreciate it.

There are other types of people who *think* they're doing you a favor but, in fact, hamper your efforts to find a job. They raise your expectations but then leave you hanging because they don't say *no*, but they never say *yes*, so they're really saying *no*. These people are very friendly. They'll talk to you at length, both on the phone and in person. But during the interview, you'll quickly realize that they don't have anything to offer you. They don't have the courage to tell you they have nothing to offer, and think they are doing you a favor by being polite. They only gave you an appointment because you asked for one. These meetings are a complete waste of time, and you'll wonder why these people even bothered to schedule them.

Then there's the person who is friendly on the telephone, talks to you at length, but won't schedule an appointment, instead saying, "Send me something in the mail, so I can look it over." Your purpose in calling is to get an appointment, not to get permission to send something, so beware of this trap. Ninety-nine percent of the time this ploy is really a brush-off. When you follow up, you'll discover that the lead is a dead end.

The other extreme is the person who answers the phone and emphatically states, "I can't talk to you; just send me something in the mail and I'll look at it." This type of person won't even give you a moment to explain why you're calling or what you want. My advice generally is to throw this name away as quickly as possible and find someone else to call.

Should you decide to mail your package of information anyway, you can expect something like this to happen. When you follow up, you'll discover you're unable to get through on the telephone. This person is always in meetings, on the telephone, or out of the office, and won't return your call; so you call again and again. When you finally get through, you're told, "I'm not interested."

These people will make you furious. You'll find yourself asking the same question over and over: "Why did you ask me to send something when you had no interest in talking to me?" These people weren't being honest. They were giving you a brush-off. With time and practice, you'll quickly be able to separate the people who are interested from the ones who don't have the guts to say *no*.

But finally you'll speak with somebody who will say, "Come on over." There will be a tone of voice that sounds different. When you meet, you will hit it off, and you'll say to yourself, "Bingo." Soon you will have gotten yourself a job.

Cold Calling Made Easy

When you're cold calling a company, contact the firm in two stages. First call and ask who the president is and how to correctly spell his or her name. If you are

asked why you're calling, just say you're sending a
letter. Don't go into any more detail. Don't ask if the
president is available, and don't attempt to get any
further information with this call.

Call again on the following day, and this time ask
for the president by name:

"Is Ms. _____ available?"

You phrase the question this way because you want
the person answering the phone to provide you with
information before you're asked to identify yourself
and the purpose of your call. If the answer is no, ask,

"Do you know when she will be available?"

If you are then told she's in a meeting, ask,

"Will she be tied up all morning (or all day)?"

If you are instead told that she's on the telephone, ask,

"Do you think it will be a long or a short call?"

If the person begins to ask questions about who you
are and what you want, ask politely,

"With whom am I speaking?"

If it's the receptionist, ask for the president's secretary
or assistant. You want to avoid being screened by the
receptionist. Receptionists are trained to say no to
everybody, but do write down the name for future
reference. Always be friendly and have the sound of a

smile in your voice. At this point it would probably be best to end the call. Do this by saying,

"Thank you very much. I'll just try a bit later."

If you decide to speak with the president's secretary, once again ask,

"Is Ms. _____ available?"

When asked who's calling, state your name but don't volunteer any additional information unless it's specifically requested. If asked the purpose or nature of your call, explain why you're calling. For example:

"I'm interested in learning more about your type of business/industry, and was wondering if Ms. _____ would be available to spare a few minutes and talk with me?"

"We met the other day at _____, and I thought her business sounded interesting. Would she be available to spare a few minutes and talk with me about it?"

"I'm a friend of _____, and he thought Ms. _____ might possibly be interested in meeting me. Would she be available for a few minutes to talk with me?"

Always be humble, and always try to make friends with the secretary. This is the person who will put your call through to the boss. A secretary may be able to provide you with information about the organization and may even be able to get you an interview.

Answer any questions directly and frankly.

The results of this interaction may vary:

- The secretary may put your call through or state that the president is not available and suggest you call later.
- The secretary may refer you to someone else at the firm.
- The secretary could put you off. If you feel dismissed, either ask if there is someone else within the firm with whom you could speak, or try to determine if the boss is just having a busy day and whether it would be better to try at some future time.

If the secretary won't put you through or the boss won't take your call, it's time to move on.

Track People Down

Don't expect to leave your phone number and have your calls returned. If you want to talk to people, it's your responsibility to reach them. Secretaries are trained to be polite and tell you,

"Mr. _____ is in a meeting but will be happy to return your call as soon as he returns."

We all know the truth. He's probably not going to return your call.

If the secretary's friendly, try to find out when the president will be available to take your call. Ask,

"Is he in meetings all day?"
"Will he be available tomorrow morning?"
"Should I try after lunch?"

Jot down a few notes to yourself on your prospect cards as a reminder of your conversation, and attempt to call again during the suggested time. Try to find out if the president comes in early, or stays late, or has a direct telephone number. Maybe you'll be able to get through at 7:00 A.M., before meetings generally start, or before the secretary has arrived.

You'll find you're doing a lot of work, much of which will seem futile, and you'll feel like you're wasting your time. But in reality you're searching for that needle in a haystack. Every time you talk with someone you'll obtain a bit more information that puts you a step or two closer to finding the job you want. It's been my experience over the years that the last call I make at the end of the day always seems to be the one that creates the most opportunities.

Deliver Your Pitch

When you finally get through, say,

"Hi, Ms. _____, thank you for taking my call. My name is X. Do you have a moment?"

This question is important because it lets her know that you realize you're taking some of her time, and don't want to interrupt her if she's in the middle of a meeting or an important project. If she can't talk, offer to call later, saying,

"May I call you later this morning (this afternoon, tomorrow), or would sometime next week be better?"

You want the conversation to start off on a positive note, with an affirmative response such as,

"Yes, I've got a few moments."

Now begin your speech:

"The reason I'm calling is . . ."

Go into detail about the purpose and nature of your call. Did you meet her at a luncheon last week? Do you have a mutual acquaintance? Did you read about her in a newspaper or magazine article? Did you work together years ago? This is the moment you've been preparing for. You now know enough about what you want, and what you have to offer, to present yourself in the best light and ask for an interview. Go for it!

8
The Interview Process

When you're interviewing for a new job, there are many factors to take into consideration in addition to the compensation package. Look at the organization as a whole. You join individuals, not companies, and it's the people within the company who make it run. In addition, before you walk through the door for your first interview, you should have a pretty good idea of what you want: the type of job, the kind of work environment, the type of relationship with your immediate supervisor, and, finally, the compensation package. This is what you were describing when you wrote the story (in your *My Ideal Job* file) about how you visualized yourself working at your new job.

The interview process usually consists of a series of meetings. These might include an initial screening interview by a personnel manager followed by interviews with your future boss and possibly your co-workers. Try to meet many different people in order to provide yourself with a broader perspective of the organization.

Your initial interviewer will probably be the personnel manager, whose role is to screen applicants by comparing their qualifications with those required for the open position, to sell qualified individuals on the benefits of joining the company, and eventually to introduce the applicant to the person who will ultimately make the hiring decision.

This first interview is your chance to find out about the position and the company, but the most important interview will be the one that takes place when you meet your future boss. The interview process gives you the opportunity to interview the company at the same time they're interviewing you. In the end, you get to decide whether or not to accept their offer.

No two interviews are alike and not every interview will lead to a job offer. Some of your interviews will seem to go on forever. The conversation drags and you realize finally that it isn't going to result in a job offer. Others will have a wonderful flow and momentum, and move forward in a very positive way. This type of interview often leads to a job offer.

Your objective is to convince the interviewers that you're the best candidate for this job, and you do it by answering their questions openly, honestly, and candidly. You've only got a few minutes to convince people that your skills, talents, and experience will help their organization solve a problem. So make the most of them.

Research Each Prospective Employer

Learn about the company before your first interview. You want to obtain some information prior to your interview so you can decide if this is a company for which you would like to work.

If the company is publicly owned, obtain a copy of its annual and quarterly reports. If the company is privately held, perhaps you could obtain copies of its sales brochures or catalogs. Call the company and ask the receptionist to send you this information. When you receive it, in addition to reading the material, study the pictures—they could give you a good idea of what the work environment looks like and even tip you off as to how you should dress for your interview. Is everyone wearing dark blue suits and "power ties" or are they dressed in jeans and polo shirts?

There are a number of places you can go to find information about both public and private companies: the business reference section of your library, the placement office at your local college, and the State Department of Labor. Many company- and industry-specific books have been published. You can also study back issues of newspapers, magazines, and industry trade journals. Finally, contact your attorney, banker, accountant, or stock broker. They or someone they know may be familiar with companies you are interested in.

During your interview, let the interviewer know that you took the time to research the company. Even if you were unable to locate any information, tell the interviewer where you went, who you talked with, and which publications you looked through, thus displaying your sincere interest in getting this job.

Crunch the Numbers

When studying financial reports, look for red flags. The most important criterion is cash flow. A business can be very profitable on paper, but if it isn't getting paid on time, it may be in trouble. A tip-off would be any major changes in accounts receivable, inventories, or cash positions. If the receivables and inventories are going up and cash is going down, there may be problems. The company could be growing too fast to keep up with the volume of business, or it can't move its products and sales are declining. Obviously a company that doesn't make a profit isn't a healthy place to work.

Read the footnotes carefully. There could be information about the firm's executive compensation and retirement plans, pending litigation, unusual business transactions, or other miscellaneous but important information that could affect your decision to take a job.

Avoid joining an organization that clearly has problems or is going through difficult times. Stay away from firms that are cutting back or laying off employees. Even if you're able to get written guarantees, they may not be worth the paper they're written on.

Prepare for the Interview

The most important part of finding a job is not the interview. It's your preparation for the interview, and you start by knowing yourself. Go back and study all those folders you compiled for preparing your resume. Familiarize yourself with what you wrote and with every item on your resume—your accomplishments, skills, abilities, and practical knowledge. Go back and review all the additional information you accumulated about yourself and what you want in a new job and career so everything is fresh in your mind.

Make a list of the toughest, most difficult, or most embarrassing questions you think you might be asked, as well as any questions you would ask if you were the interviewer. Write out and practice your answers.

Most of us have at least one or two problem spots in our employment history, such as a demotion, a period of unemployment, or a position from which we were fired. If you do, be prepared to explain the situation and circumstances frankly and succinctly. If you start to hem and haw or squirm like a worm on a hook when difficult questions are asked, the interview will be over! If you've got a black mark on your record, find a way to deal with it and turn your answer into a positive response. If you've had problems in the past, don't lie about them now. Sooner or later the truth will come out, and when it does your credibility or even your career will be damaged.

Plan to explain in detail what you have to offer this company and why you want to work for them. Convince them to hire you. Talk about the major contributions you've made to your previous employers and emphasize the transferability of your skills to this industry or firm. Point out the commitments you've made to prior projects, explain why you're capable of doing this job, and describe how you will bring to it a high level of energy and motivation. Tell stories that highlight your motivation and dedication. Take advantage of every opportunity to talk about and discuss the results that you and your employers achieved as a result of your hard work and effort.

Describe your management style and why you consider yourself a good manager. Be prepared to discuss what you feel are the most challenging parts of being a manager. If you're familiar with this company's particular industry, talk about the direction you see the industry going.

Anticipate questions about your former employer and your working relationship with your supervisor, manager, or boss. If you find yourself discussing unpleasant or difficult experiences, don't allow your emotions to get the best of you, and don't display any feelings of anger. *Never* say anything bad about your former employer or supervisor during a job interview.

Your ability to answer questions stems from your advance preparation for the interview. You also have the opportunity to pose questions during the meeting. Review your lists and think about what you're looking for in your ideal job. What points are most important to you? Write the list of questions that you would like to ask about the company, about the boss, and about the job itself. Bring the list with you, and don't be afraid to pull it out, put it on the desk, and refer to it. You will impress your interviewer because you are thorough, detailed, and have done your homework.

Polish Your Answers

Your job is to convince a skeptical buyer that your qualifications are real. The product you're selling is yourself, and you must be convincing. Several days before your interview, begin your practice sessions. Practice talking about yourself and answering questions, and try to imagine what the interview will be like. Don't forget to review your list of power verbs and power adjectives that describe you.

While you're going through your rehearsal, use your notes and play with the presentation of your answers. Try to be serious one time, and then answer the same question as if you're telling a funny story and can't keep a straight face before getting to the punch line. This is an excellent technique for taking the nervousness out of your voice and learning to speak in a more natural, conversational tone. Walk around the room, relax, have some fun, and pretend you're an actor on stage. It's important to maintain eye contact during the interview, so practice focusing on different objects in the room, imagining that they are the faces of people interviewing you, and don't forget to practice in front of a mirror to see how you look.

During other practice sessions, answer questions while you're sitting at a desk or table. Be aware that when you're seated your energy level drops. So work to maintain the same high level of enthusiasm you have when you're standing. Of course you'll be nervous—your heart will be pounding, the palms of your hands will be sweaty, and your throat will be dry. Try to relax. When you speak, your voice should project power, authority, and confidence. This can only be done when your lungs are filled with air.

Make it a habit to take a deep breath before you answer a question or make a statement. This has two important benefits: it provides you with an extra moment to think about what you want to say, and it gives you the time to fill your lungs so you can speak more easily. Remember to smile while you're talking. Be aware of your hand and body movements. Make gestures occasionally, but don't wave your hands wildly or fidget with items on the desk. To keep your hands under control, try clasping your fingers together from time to time.

Give your list of questions to a family member or a close friend and have them role-play with you. Tape-record the sessions and critique yourself afterward. Practice your answers so everything is at the tip of your tongue; then, when you are asked any question, you'll be prepared with an appropriate response. With practice you'll be able to answer any and every question with honesty and candor, even the hard ones.

Recognize Inappropriate Lines of Questioning

Illegal Questions

There are a number of questions an interviewer has no legal right to ask, but might still broach due to his or her own inexperience. Good jobs are in short supply, and even when you know you shouldn't answer a certain question, you may be placed—unintentionally—in an uncomfortable position because you're afraid the context of the interview will change and you won't get the job.

Most people applying for jobs have had limited experience of going through the interview process.

Unless you've been coached on how to respond to an illegal or inappropriate question, it's easy to accidentally disqualify yourself as a suitable candidate by inadvertently volunteering information about yourself that is not job-related. You want to follow a defensive strategy when answering questions so you won't remove yourself from consideration as a potential employee because you offered too much personal information.

As you answer questions, volunteer nothing about your personal life. Respond to each question with specific facts and information. You don't have to answer any question that isn't job-related. Think about how each question relates to either the company or the position for which you're applying. Unless asked for specific information, don't offer it. Limit your conversation to a discussion of each part of the job and talk only about your ability to perform that job. You are there to explain how your qualifications make you a suitable candidate for this position. Interviewers want to hear candidates talk, so talk at length about all the reasons you're qualified to fill this position.

EEOC Guidelines

There are lines of questioning that the federal and state governments and the courts have determined to be discriminatory. These improper questions have been outlined by the Equal Employment Opportunity Commission (EEOC). Questions that maintain a job-related focus are not in violation of EEOC guidelines.

Category	Illegal or Discriminatory Questions	Acceptable Questions
Age	How old are you?	None
Arrest Record	Have you ever been arrested?	None
Birthplace and Nationality	Where were you born? Where were your parents born? What is the national origin of your name?	Have you ever worked under another name?
Citizenship	Where were you born? Are you a naturalized citizen?	Are you a citizen of the U.S. or do you have a visa that permits you to work here? (You must furnish proof of such if hired.)
Education	Do you have a high school diploma or college degree? (If not job-related)	OK if job-related
English Language Skill	Can you read/write/speak English? (If not job-related)	OK if job-related
Financial Status	Do you own your own home? Have you ever filed for bankruptcy?	None
Friends or Relatives Working for the Same Employer	Do you have any friends or relatives working for our company?	How did you hear about this job opportunity?
Height and Weight	How tall are you? How much do you weigh?	None

Category	Illegal or Discriminatory Questions	Acceptable Questions
Marital Status	What is your marital status?	None
Military Service	Under what circumstances were you discharged from the military?	What type of work experience or training did you receive in the military?
Number of Children	How many children do you have? Do you plan any additions to your family? What contraceptive practices do you use?	None
Personal Information	Have you changed your name through an application in court or marriage?	Have you ever worked for our organization under your name or another name?
Provisions for Child Care	What arrangements have you made for child care?	None
Race or Color	What color is your skin/eyes/hair?	None
Religion or Creed	What is your religious denomination/ affiliation/church? Who is your pastor? What religious holidays do you observe?	None
Sex	What are your sexual preferences?	None

Questions About Salary

In the early stages of the interviewing process, try to avoid a discussion of your salary expectations or compensation history. Most people prefer that salary and compensation discussions take place just before an offer is made, once the interviewer is sold on your outstanding qualifications. When posed earlier, often as a screening technique, these questions can put you in an uncomfortable position. You're afraid that a wrong answer—stating a salary that's either too high or too low, for example—will alienate the interviewer and remove you from consideration. Your sole objective at this stage is to convince the interviewer that you have the ability to do the job. A discussion about salary will take away from the time you have available to tell your story.

Should you be asked a question about your salary expectations or compensation history, there are a number of factors to take into consideration before responding. What has been the tone, flavor, or chemistry of the meeting up until this point? Has the interview been going well? What questions were asked just prior to the one about your salary history? Was the line of questions leading in this direction, or did this question come out of left field? If the interview wasn't going in the right direction, this is a good indication that it's over. The interviewer is looking for a reason to pass you over as a candidate.

There are several ways to respond to this question, but there are no right or wrong answers. You're doing the best you can under what will certainly be uncomfortable circumstances.

- You can give a specific answer stating how much you've earned in each of the past two or three years.
- You can give a salary range over the same period of time.
- You can suggest that you talk more and postpone the discussion about salary until you've covered some other items.

Negative Lines of Questioning

Another uncomfortable situation arises when you're asked to talk about your weak points or shortcomings. This is a negative line of questioning and may be another indication that the interview isn't going well. You don't want to start talking about any weak points because you just might be talking yourself out of a job. Try to change the flow of the conversation. Respond by saying something like,

> "We all have areas in need of improvement. Of course there are things I want to learn to do even better, but let me tell you about some of the things I really do well. I think that would be more meaningful and important to you. Let me tell you about . . ."

Unethical Questions

If your interviewer, even unintentionally, asks for confidential or proprietary information concerning any of your former employers, you are being placed in a very uncomfortable position. You're there because you want a job, you want to be cooperative, and you certainly don't want to be confrontational. Before you respond, ask yourself why this question is being asked, and what the intent or relevance of the question is.

A few companies may actually use a job interview as an opportunity to attempt to debrief you of confidential or proprietary information. They have no interest in hiring you. (Even if you think they might extend an offer, what kinds of things could they ask you to do after you start working there if they're already asking unethical questions during the job interview?) A red flag is being raised, and you should proceed with caution from this point forward. Try to politely and calmly explain that this is a confidential subject you're unable to discuss. Should the interviewer persist, terminate the conversation. This company's ethical standards don't meet yours. You may also want to ask your attorney about what information you're free to discuss during interviews with a new employer.

Make a Great First Impression

Your interview begins when you wake up in the morning and start getting dressed. Your clothing should be appropriate to the business environment, your appearance immaculate—your suit freshly pressed, shirt starched, shoes polished, fingernails and hair neatly groomed. A man should wear a white shirt with a dark suit, and a woman should wear a business suit or dress, not a skirt or a pair of slacks. (Do not wear dressy jewelry unless you're interviewing for a position in the fashion or beauty industry and feel wearing it would be appropriate for the job for which you're applying.)

When you walk through the company's front door, be polite, friendly, and personable to everybody. Display all your social skills. For all you know, the person who walked in the door with you is your prospective boss, your interviewer, or the company president. You *must* be on time. If you can arrive ten minutes early you'll make an even better impression. If you arrive late, you're already starting on a bad note. Ask to use the washroom before you're announced. Take this opportunity to freshen up and comb your hair.

The first three minutes of any interview are critical. You never have a second chance to make a first impression. If you're carrying a briefcase, carry it in your left hand so that when you introduce yourself, you're able to shake hands with your right hand.

Go with the Flow

You won't be able to control the interview or even predict how it will go, so don't be overly concerned. Be flexible, go with the flow, and try your best to fully express and communicate your ideas with everyone you meet. No matter how much time you've spent in preparation, sometimes an interview goes well and other times it's a disaster, so don't expect every interview to go smoothly or have favorable results. Every interview has a life of its own, and you'll find yourself adapting the points you've rehearsed to a variety of questions and interviewer styles. You can only hope that a good rapport will develop between you and the interviewer, but sometimes this is beyond your control.

If an interview isn't going well, don't get angry or become aggressive or overly demonstrative. It isn't the end of the world. Once these things start going downhill, it's very difficult to change their direction. In this situation, don't overstay your welcome or prolong the agony. End the interview quickly, say how much you appreciated their taking the time to meet with you, and exit gracefully.

Eventually every interview reaches a critical decision point. Will a job be offered? If offered, will you accept it? If the answer to either of these questions is *no*, it's time to leave, go home, get back on the phone, and schedule more interviews.

Interview Your Future Boss

Your job responsibilities will be determined by your immediate supervisor. You're attempting at this stage to determine how well the two of you will work together. This is your opportunity to ask questions, so take advantage of it. You can learn a great deal about your future boss by paying close attention to how you feel inside and to your gut reactions during your conversations:

- How does he ask you questions?
- How does he listen when you speak?
- How does he respond to your questions, statements, or responses to questions?

Ask about his career. How long has he been with the firm? What positions has he previously held? Where has he worked in the past? (In the back of your mind you're also asking yourself, "Is he on the move? What is the likelihood he'll still be here during the next three to five years?") Would a change in his position have an impact on your career?

Ask him about his management skills. Which of them does he feel serve him best? What is his preferred style of communication within the office? Does he prefer to hold regular staff meetings, impromptu meetings, or send memos back and forth? How available will he be when you need an answer to a question or help in solving a problem? How much time will be spent in training you? What will be expected of you as a new employee?

You will want to find out, of course, what skills a future supervisor feels are necessary to adequately handle the responsibilities of this position as well as get a feel for what is expected of you in the way of the number of hours you will spend at the office. Is this a company where you'll be expected to be at your desk at 7:30 A.M. and work beyond 5:00 P.M., where last-minute unexpected rush projects are the norm rather than the exception? Will you be expected to work weekends? Does the company have a policy of flexible work hours?

The condition of a supervisor's office can tell you a great deal about how he or she conducts business. What does the office look like? Is it meticulous and organized, or does the desk look like a toxic waste dump? How much time do you think is wasted looking for letters, memos, and files—and how often do you suspect you'll be needed, at the very last minute, to take care of something that's become a crisis because it was lost? Does there appear to be a lot of unfinished work lying around? How thick is the pile of unreturned pink phone messages? Should you be offered the job, this could indicate an opportunity to let your habits of efficient organization shine.

How considerate is your future boss of your time? Was the door closed during your meeting? Were telephone calls forwarded? Did he allow people to walk into the office and interrupt the interview? How thoroughly did he take notes?

Before the interview ends, you should ask two more questions.

> "What else can I tell you about myself or my career experiences that we have not discussed?"
> "What would be your assessment of this interview?"

You want to take this final opportunity to clear up any misunderstandings that could hurt your chances of getting this job, and with these final questions you'll know exactly where you stand and that nothing important has been overlooked.

And, finally, listen to your gut. What are you feeling inside? Are you relaxed, comfortable, and at ease or are you nervous and tense? Has the interview left you impressed, inspired, and enthused? Are you excited about the prospect of working for this company?

As the meeting is ending, ask what the next step in the process will be and the time schedule for making a decision. As you're saying good-bye, pull out a fresh copy of your resume and marketing package to leave behind.

Meet Some Other Employees

If possible, ask for the opportunity to speak with other employees in addition to the original interviewer and your future boss. Ideally you would like to meet peers, support staff, and other people in your new work area. These are the people who will become your colleagues, coworkers, and friends. Try to talk with them privately for a few minutes at their desks or during a coffee break. Perhaps you could join them for lunch.

Your purpose in meeting with these people is to discover how they feel about their careers, the company, the industry, and their boss. Ask about the firm's major competitors and how business has been. (If you don't take this position, you could possibly call one of the competitors.) Can you get a feel about where the management of the company puts its emphasis? Is the company investing in both the company's and the employees' futures, or does management seem more preoccupied with the next quarter's financial results and its stock price? Does management encourage employees to work together as members of a team, or as individuals? Do the employees appear to have pride in the organization?

Try to glean opinions and observations about your future boss. What do they see as his leadership skills? How does he go about motivating and inspiring his colleagues and staff to produce their best work? Is this the kind of person they would do anything for?

Do You Like What You See?

During your interviews try to observe how other people are treated. How sensitive do employees appear to be toward the needs of coworkers? How do they talk to one another or address each other in the hallways? Are they warm, cordial, and friendly or abrupt and sarcastic? How do they respond to strangers in the waiting room or reception area? Do they appear to be having fun? Is there laughter in the hallways? How do they treat you?

Take notes during your meetings and conversations, and be sure to jot down your comments and feelings when the interviews have been completed. What is your gut reaction to the people you've met? Would you enjoy working with them? How does the company's value system compare to yours? Remember, you're interviewing them while they're interviewing you, and *you* get to decide if this is where you want to work.

Evaluate the Job Offer

After all your hard work and effort, the time finally comes when you're offered a job. Now you must decide if you want to accept it. The first thing you should always do is thank your prospective employer for extending an offer and say how pleased you are. But the extension of an offer is just the beginning of the negotiating process. Even if you say yes on the spot, there will probably be a number of items that need to be discussed before you and your new employer have a meeting of the minds and are able to agree on all the specific terms of your employment.

Give yourself a day or two to think about the offer. Make a list of everything you like about it and what you'd like to change. Your decision whether or not to accept the offer will be much easier when you are clear about what you want and what's most important to you. (If you're having difficulty deciding which parts of the employment package mean the most to you, refer to the priority comparisons on page

29.) How does this offer compare to your ideal job? In what areas does it provide you with more than you could ever want? In what areas does it provide you with less?

Once you decide to accept an offer, the odds are pretty good that you'll be able to come to an agreement on all the major and minor points of discussion. Almost everything in a job offer is negotiable, with a few exceptions: company-wide health and welfare benefits, for example, and tax-preferred programs such as pension and profit-sharing plans. You will certainly have some specific questions about the new job:

- Will you be provided with a written job description outlining your day-to-day duties and responsibilities?
- Who will you be reporting to on a daily basis?
- What criteria will be used to evaluate your performance? Will this be done formally (written), or informally (orally)? How frequently will performance evaluations take place? Who will perform the appraisals?
- When should you arrive at work (as opposed to when *must* you be at work)? For example, starting time is 8:30 A.M., but almost everybody is at their desks and working by 8:00. This could be important if you are a parent with children in day care and you must make alternative arrangements if it's necessary to arrive at the office early in the morning.

This should be discussed as part of the employment package, after a job has been offered. (During the interview stage, a prospective employer cannot ask about your marital status, whether you're pregnant, what your plans for having children are, or the number and ages of your children.)

Ask for a copy of the firm's employee manual or policy and procedure handbook. This will answer many of your specific questions, especially in cases where your immediate supervisor may not be well versed in all the details of the company's personnel benefits.

When you get to the discussion about your compensation package, you may find that the company is limited by tenure policies or fixed salary ranges as to what they can offer for your starting salary, but perhaps you can negotiate a salary plus performance bonus. Should that be the case, you'll need a written agreement stating how the bonus will be calculated and paid. You may discover that your new employer can also be flexible with these other items:

- Amount of vacation time
- Extra travel time for holidays
- Frequency of raises
- Stock options
- The amount of group or supplemental life insurance

- Salary continuation plans in the event of death or disability
- Terms of an exit contract in the event of termination
- Relocation benefits

When your requests are reasonable, almost anything can be negotiated. First offers are rarely final offers. There will be certain parts of the package that aren't open to further discussion, but a great deal of flexibility may be available in other parts. You want to foster an open and friendly atmosphere where you can talk candidly and honestly. You want the job they're offering, they want you to have it, and you're both looking for that happy medium. You'll give on some points, and they'll give on others. You're trying to create a win-win situation.

In order to avoid any future misunderstandings, once your negotiations have concluded, everything you have agreed on should be put in writing.

Family-oriented corporate policies and programs have become an important issue for many people. Job seekers are now insisting on a balance between career and family, and want to work for employers that are supportive of family needs. Some of the programs and benefits companies are beginning to offer include child-care centers, maternity/paternity leave, time off to care for ill relatives, flexible scheduling, job sharing, and the opportunity to work at home. If any of these issues are important to you, don't hesitate to bring them up for discussion after you have been offered a job.

What if You Are Hesitant?

What is the specific reason that makes you hesitate to say yes? How does this job offer compare to your ideal job? What do you want that they're not providing? Do you have concerns about the job description, the travel schedule, the commuting time, the company's health, the compensation or benefits package? These are all legitimate considerations that you'll need to think over before making a decision.

Make a list of all the reasons why you think you *should* take the job. Then make a second list of the things you want in a job that are *lacking* in this position. Compare the two lists, and if you think they could be fairly easily resolved, discuss specific concerns with your future employer to see if it's possible to remove your doubts and come to a mutually acceptable agreement

Measuring One Offer Against Another

If you're offered a job but you're hoping another offer will be forthcoming, never mention the latter. You want the employer who's made you a concrete offer to feel special. This is like dating—if you talk about the other people you're seeing, the person you're going out with will lose interest in you *fast*. Discussing another company is in very bad taste and may ruin your opportunities with this company.

The first thing to do is thank them for extending their offer and tell them how pleased you are, but explain that you'll need a little bit of time to think about it before making a decision. Ask how much time you could have—one day? Two days? Three days?

You must decide quickly why the other offer, if extended, would be more appealing. Would they pay you more money? Are the benefits better? Is the position more attractive? Would you hesitate accepting this first offer if there weren't a second company to consider? You may want to contact this second company and mention that you've received a job offer and must make your decision within a few days. See how they respond. Do they offer you the job immediately or are they unable to make a quick decision? You don't want to lose the first offer and then discover the second one falls through too.

These situations aren't easy. Instead of worrying about making the *best* decision, would you be making a *good* decision if you were to accept the first offer? If that's the case, accept the offer.

Always get back with your response to the person who offered you the job before the agreed-upon deadline. If you're late you may discover the offer has been withdrawn. Many employers will confirm their offer in writing, stating that it will remain open until a specific date and then will be withdrawn. You don't want to frustrate your potential employer's quest to fill an open position.

9
Make the Most of Your New Job

Congratulations!

You deserve a big pat on the back and a hearty round of applause for a job well done. You've gone out and found yourself a new job. Now you're faced with another challenge—to show your new boss that she not only made a good decision, she made a great one. You need to learn how to do your new job and strive to produce the highest-quality work, doing it quickly and efficiently.

Get the Details Right

Rather than looking only at the definition of your new job, try to pinpoint exactly what you want to accomplish, and look at the process of how you go about doing your work. When you get the details right, the results take care of themselves. Concentrate on how and why things happen instead of focusing on the result. When you're able to improve the processes, the work goes more smoothly and you become more productive.

Pay more attention to what you do during the course of a day and you'll discover new ways to accomplish more work in less time with less effort. Strive to produce the highest-quality work and pay close attention to the issues or projects that need to be addressed today. Ask yourself:

- What new ideas can come from these daily activities?
- Is there a better way to do this work?
- What is the *best* way for me to do this work?

Success doesn't come overnight. It takes time to develop new ideas and improve business skills. The objective is to continue moving forward, one small step at a time.

Organize Your New Work Load

Keep a Master List of things to do, and keep track of all your unfinished work and upcoming projects so you won't lose track of anything. Carry on with the habits of organizing tasks that you developed during your job search.

Schedule Appointments with Yourself

When you have an important project that needs your undivided time and attention, schedule an appointment with yourself and write it on the calendar. Close the door and turn off the telephone so you won't be interrupted, and go to work.

Give Yourself the First Two Hours of the Day

Get your most important work done early in the day, before the fires flare up and your whole day goes up in smoke. Try to keep the morning open until at least 10:30 or 11:00 A.M. Don't schedule any meetings during that time. Don't take any phone calls. Don't allow yourself to be interrupted. You'll find you complete twice as much work in half the time with half the effort.

Set Your Career Timetable

In planning the rest of your career, give yourself enough time to grow into your present position, and then begin to prepare yourself for that next career move. Expand your network of professional contacts, because it's quite likely you'll be changing jobs again within the next three to five years. Set realistic timetables for yourself. When thinking about that next job, try to determine what the new position will demand of you and begin preparing yourself for those demands today. Continue to work at improving your skills and qualifications. Think about what you need to do, and set up a plan and work out a timetable to accomplish your career goals.

Look for a Mentor

Learn from people who have been there before. Take advantage of your boss's knowledge, training, and expertise. And find a mentor, a role model, a person who will take you under his or her wing, giving you guidance and direction. You'll speed up the learning process and your career will move along at a faster pace.

Study how your mentor deals with ideas, communicates with people, and makes decisions. You'll learn a great deal simply by listening and observing. You'll quickly identify key players, begin to understand the politics of the organization, and learn how to maneuver within the system.

Build Your Business Relationships

Your career with your new employer will flourish when you interact with people in a positive way and deal with them fairly and honestly. We all have different kinds of personal skills, and by learning how to take advantage of our special talents, we can easily improve our professional relationships. Work on improving your communication skills so that you're able to express your point of view in a positive, informative, and convincing way to colleagues and co-workers.

When you express yourself effectively your leadership skills improve, you motivate others, and everyone produces better work. You increase your opportunities to make a big contribution to the organization.

Create a positive communication network around yourself—a good flow of information can be very helpful to your career. You may hear of new career opportunities before other people do when you've established rapport with your coworkers.

People need to be encouraged, nurtured with positive reinforcement, made to feel important, and told that their hard work and effort is appreciated. Make other people feel valued and do things that will further their careers. Bring everybody together and let them know you're all working toward a common goal. Acknowledge them for their contributions. Give them praise and a big pat on the back for a job well done.

Reduce the Stress in Your Life

Everyone has stress, but if you can reduce the number of stressful events in your life and find constructive ways to eliminate the daily buildup of tensions and emotions, you'll make your life easier. Excess stress can destroy a career.

Here are some of the reasons why businesspeople have too much stress:

- They're working at jobs they don't like.
- They've taken positions beyond their abilities, skills, or technical knowledge.
- They're perfectionists who are never satisfied with their accomplishments.
- They've become too emotionally involved in their work.
- They try to do too much work in too short a time, and run out of gas.
- They insist on doing everything themselves instead of utilizing the resources available.
- They say *yes* whenever they're asked to take on more projects without giving

adequate consideration to the commitments they've already made.

There are things you can do to reduce the stress in your life. Take a few minutes between projects to relax and recharge your batteries and allow yourself to calm down at the end of the day. Establish a more sustainable pace and your career will be much smoother and more enjoyable. Don't push yourself so hard that you break down. Your business career may span forty years, so if you go full out, day after day, you'll burn out. Work to relieve the stress in your life, and you'll discover the quality of your work improves while you're putting in fewer hours at the office.

A good sense of humor is your first line of defense against stress. Don't take everything so seriously. There is relatively little in life that we can truly control, and when we quit attempting to do so we can reduce our stress levels. Counteract the forces that cause stress by participating in activities that calm you down and make you feel better.

Here are some additional ways you can reduce the level of stress in your life:

- *Keep a neat office.* At the end of the day, give yourself time to relax and unwind, start planning for tomorrow, and clean up your desk.
- *Take a siesta.* A ten-to-fifteen-minute break for a stress-reducing siesta can be very relaxing and energizing.
- *Eat lunch.* You'll be much more relaxed and less irritable when you take the time to eat lunch every day.

- *Cool off at the office.* When you get excited or upset, give yourself time to cool off and pull yourself back together. When you get angry, count to ten; if you're very angry, count to a hundred.
- *Treat yourself to a massage.* A massage is a wonderful way to relax and rejuvenate tired muscles and remove the physical stress, strain, and tension from your body.
- *Eat dinner with your family.* Eating dinner together provides a peaceful respite from the frenzy of the day and brings the family together.
- *Sleep more.* Studies have shown that mental alertness and job performance are reduced when you don't get enough sleep. With a full night's sleep you're less irritable and are better prepared to deal with whatever comes your way.
- *Start exercising.* Physical exercise helps you release built-up tension, takes your mind off your problems, and allows you to relax. Play racquetball or tennis, go swimming, running, or jogging, even walk the dog. Do anything that uses your muscles. You'll feel mentally refreshed and physically invigorated when you're finished.
- *Get organized.* People who are too busy to get organized don't have time to do anything well. They run around in a constant tizzy, going from one crisis to another, without ever taking the time to

solve the problems that are increasing at a geometric rate. Slow down. Identify and work on the important, meaningful projects, the ones that will have a big payoff. Eliminate the projects and activities that just waste time. These keep you busy but hardly productive.

- *Get more out of life.* Become involved in more activities outside the office. Allow yourself the pleasure of pursuing your hobbies. Would you like to play the piano, take painting classes, work in the garden, or bake bread? Become involved in a variety of activities. You'll enrich your life and make yourself a more well-rounded individual.

And finally, move out of stressful situations before they get the best of you—take a long weekend every few months, and take a vacation at least once or twice during the year.

Relax at Your Desk

There are several stretching exercises you can do while you're sitting at your desk. These will help you to relax and remove some of the tension and strain from your body:

- *Breathing*—While sitting, focus on your breathing. Inhale through your nose and exhale through your mouth. Breathe deeply from your diaphragm. Feel your chest expand as it fills up with air. As you exhale, add a gentle sigh, and allow your arms, neck, and head to go limp. Feel your whole body relax. Repeat several times.

- *Shoulders*—Sit up straight, hold your head high, and roll your shoulders back five or six times, then forward five or six times.
- *Shoulder blades and back*—Sit up straight, clasp your hands behind your head, and squeeze your shoulder blades together. Take a deep breath, and as you exhale, allow your muscles to relax.
- *Neck*—Straighten and arch your back. Sit up straight and hold your head high. Relax your neck by tilting your head and try to gently touch your right ear to your right shoulder, stretching the muscles on the left side of your neck. Let your head roll forward so your chin touches your chest, rest a moment, and lift up your head again. Now try to touch your left ear to your left shoulder, and let your head roll forward again, rest a moment, and then lift it up. Repeat this two or three times.

Take some time throughout the day to relax for a few moments.

The Key to Success

Now that you have a complete overview of my Career Discovery System, it's time to go to work. Go back to the beginning of the book and start asking yourself some questions. The more time you allow yourself to think and search for answers, the easier it will be for you to identify and land your ideal job.

If you want professional help in selecting a career path, work with a career counselor. But remember, the degree of success you achieve will be determined by the amount of effort you put into your search to find the job that is right for you. A career counselor is not a substitute for the work you must do.

In the end, people who have found careers that utilize their skills, talents, and natural abilities to their fullest extent truly love their work. When you do the right things, you get the right results. Be enthusiastic and work hard to maintain a positive attitude. Believe that everything will work out, because you're going to make it work out. Visualize yourself doing the work you were born to do. See yourself exceeding your goals and accomplishing much more than you ever dreamed was possible. Give yourself enough time and eventually you'll succeed. Be flexible in your thinking, be willing to make changes or modify your approach when necessary, and whenever you come to a fork in the road, don't worry about which way you should choose to go. You'll know that either way will be right for you.

Do You Have Any Comments?

If you would like to share any of your experiences, offer your comments, or invite the author to address a group or organization, you may write to:

Jeffrey J. Mayer
Mayer Enterprises
50 East Bellevue Place
Chicago, Illinois 60611